WHAT FAITH REALLY MEANS

A SIMPLE EXPLANATION

BY THE

REV. HENRY GREY GRAHAM, M.A.

AUTHOR OF
"WHERE WE GOT THE BIBLE," ETC.

WITH FOREWORD BY THE

RIGHT REV. JAMES W. McCARTHY, D.D.

BISHOP OF GALLOWAY

TAN BOOKS AND PUBLISHERS, INC.
Rockford, Illinois 61105

Nihil Obstat.

C. SCHUT, S.T.D.

Censor Deputatus.

Imprimatur.

EDM. CAÑONICUS SURMONT, D.D.,

Vicarius Generalis.

WESTMONASTERII,

Die 30 Septembris, 1914.

Published by B. Herder Book Co., St. Louis, Missouri, in 1914, in cooperation with R. & T. Washbourne Limited, London.

Library of Congress Catalog Card No.: 82-74243

ISBN: 0-89555-204-3

Printed and bound in the United States of America.

TAN BOOKS AND PUBLISHERS, INC.
P.O. Box 424
Rockford, Illinois 61105

1982

FOREWORD

WHAT does Divine Faith really mean ? No one, outside the Catholic Church, can answer the question with any certainty. Something indefinite concerning God and our Lord Jesus Christ, a vague and hazy notion about the truths of religion, is all that it conveys to the non-Catholic mind. And yet it is the most important question for the souls of men: " Unless you believe you shall be condemned." What am I to believe ? is the puzzling problem that perturbs the soul of every well-disposed man and woman outside the fold of the Church. They search in vain for something certain to hold on by, and the more they search amongst the non-Catholic creeds the more they find " confusion worse confounded."

If the inquirer wants to find the Truth that comes from God, he can find it only from the Teachers and " Dispensers of the mysteries of God," appointed by Him for that special purpose.

In the natural sciences qualified teachers are appointed to unfold their mysteries to scholars and students. How particular the Senate of a university, the Committees on Secondary Education and School Boards are in examining the qualifications of a Professor or school-teacher before they appoint either to impart a knowledge of the sciences to others !

In law and medicine, as these subjects have such far-reaching effect on the rights and well-being of the people, the Government will not allow an unlicensed professor to teach students in any of their departments, nor will it permit any person to publicly practise those sciences unless the authorized corporation confers on them the requisite degrees, under the penalty of fines or imprisonment. Property and men's natural and conferred rights are too sacred to be tampered with by any unauthorized person taking upon himself to decide on those matters! The whole power of the Government of every civilized country surrounds the administrators of the law—solicitors, magistrates, judges!

It is of vital moment to the health of the communities to have qualified physicians to minister to " the ills that flesh is heir to "; hence the State, with unsheathed sword, forbids unqualified persons to practise the science of medicine, under pain of severe penalties! Now, no doubt the rights of man and the health of the people are of paramount importance, but is not the teaching of Religion the most important of all the sciences to be imparted to the people who profess Christianity? Is every person qualified to stand up in the market-place, or hall, or church, and propound the most sacred of all sciences— the Truths of Religion—no matter how profound the depths of his ignorance may be?

Medicine is an empirical natural science, law is the science of the rights of man; the knowledge of both may be acquired by any scholar, yet governments must be satisfied that the students have obtained a qualifying degree of a recognized school before they are allowed to practise amongst the people.

Is there no power to prevent the unqualified from teaching the followers of Christ unsound doctrine that will corrupt their souls ? There is the first and greatest of all powers—the power of conscience directed by God, " Who will have all men to be saved and to come to the knowledge of the Truth." He has appointed His Professors, His Teachers, his Vicars, His Representatives, His Ambassadors, His Apostles, " to go and teach whatsoever He has taught them," " until the consummation of the world." They alone are qualified, and licensed, and appointed to teach the Truths of God: " He that hears you, hears Me." To reject their teaching is to reject God's teaching: " He that despiseth you, despiseth Me."

The science of Religion is not human, therefore it does not belong to the empirical sciences, to be discovered by experimental research; but as it unfolds a knowledge of God—a pure Spirit—His attributes, and His relations with man, it is entirely beyond the powers of a finite human intellect to penetrate into His mysteries; hence man depends altogether for his knowledge of heavenly things on the revelations that God has deigned to give of Himself. Under the Old Covenant, He revealed much of Himself, through His *chosen* prophets; under the New Covenant, the second Person of the Blessed Trinity, God the Son, became man, lived amongst men, taught men with human words through human lips still more of the mysteries of Heaven. He then *chose* men to be the appointed Teachers of His revealed Truths; He breathed on them the power He possessed; He commissioned *them and their successors* to be *His only representatives*, in preaching the Gospel and administering His Sacraments until the end of time.

Find, therefore, the successors of the Apostles, and you find the only accredited, genuine ambassadors of Christ on earth. All others are spurious, all others are wolves in sheeps' clothing, leading men to spiritual destruction. To one who has grasped this all-important principle all else follows in a natural sequence. " Faith is to believe without doubting, whatever God has revealed," and since this revelation can only be known from the successors of the Apostles who reside in the Catholic Church alone, we must in consequence go to the Catholic Church to learn the true science of religion.

Whilst it is our duty to remove all obstacles that stand between us and Divine Faith, we must at the same time ever know and remember that it is a free gift of God, which He will certainly grant to us if we seek it by fervent prayer.

BISHOP OF GALLOWAY.

St. Benedict's,
   Maxwelltown,
      Dumfries.
         July 13, 1914.

PREFACE

THIS little book purports to be a simple explanation, for those who require it, of what an Act of Faith really is, and what it means, for a Catholic. As it is not a formal treatise on Faith, I have not entered into many theological distinctions familiar to students of the subject, or attempted to go very deeply into many questions raised. For example, I have not distinguished between Divine Faith, Catholic Faith, Divine-Catholic Faith; for practical purposes it all comes to the same thing; it is in any case infallible.

I should consider myself well rewarded for my trouble if I thought that a perusal of the book had led any non-Catholic to inquire farther into matters of faith, and above all into the claims of the Catholic Church to his submission as the ordinary medium of God's Revelation to mankind. Before he can accept the authority of the Catholic Church it is evident that he must first have satisfied himself in reason that it is in truth God's One True Church, commissioned to teach with Divine authority.

But though he were so convinced, something more is required before he can enter within the Fold. His will must be moved, and he must suffer it to be moved, by the grace of God. As has been well said: " Reason leads us to the door of faith, but there it leaves us." It cannot be too often repeated that Faith is a supernatural gift of God, bestowed by Him out of His good pleasure. One here, another there, receives it ; others live and die without it. Why it should be so we cannot say, except " as it is

written, Jacob have I loved, but Esau I have hated "
(Rom. ix. 13).   When all is said and done, therefore, the
gift of Faith must be offered by God, but it must also be
accepted by man with the help of God's holy grace.   For
this prayer is an absolute necessity, and all can pray, and
the good God will answer their prayer.   And once the
mind has been illumined with the Light of Faith, there will
come upon the soul a great peace and joy, born not of
this world.   The experience of a convert is like that of
one who awaits the dawn.   Midnight past, he discerns
the first streaks of daylight, and soon rejoices in the full
light of Heaven.   Thus it is when the Sun of God's Truth
bursts upon his soul: " In Thy light we shall see light "
(Ps. xxxv. 10).   This is the " reward exceeding great "
for every genuine convert.

Thanks are due to the editors of the Catholic journals
in which these papers originally appeared for permitting
their reproduction; they are here extended, and in places
corrected.

H. G. G.

Our Lady of Good Aid,
     Motherwell,
        1914.

CONTENTS

WHAT FAITH REALLY MEANS

INTRODUCTION

" How am I to know what God has revealed ?" This question in the Catechism of Christian Doctrine is really the most important question that a Christian can put to himself. It is the question of questions. Perhaps some one will say that that other question, " What must you do to save your soul ?" is more important; and at first sight it might seem so. But assuming that a man *has* determined to save his soul, the grand question for him is: " What has Almighty God revealed on the matter, and how can I get to know it ?" And at present I am supposing the case of a man who *is* anxious to be saved, who believes that " God made us to know Him, love Him, and serve Him in this world, and to be happy with Him for ever in the next "; who believes that he is endowed with an immortal soul, and that his chief concern in this world is to save that soul, and that it will profit him nothing if he gain the whole world and suffer the loss of it. I am supposing, further, that to this end he realizes the necessity of faith, as well as of hope and charity, for " without faith it is impossible to please God." He does not (I am assuming) consider it a matter of indifference what a man believes, or how he believes, or whether he believes at all, for " he that believeth not shall be condemned." He knows that Almighty God has made a Revelation on the subject, that He has revealed the Gospel of Salvation, that indeed

9

this Revelation was the sole end and purpose of the mission of Jesus Christ in the world, and that therefore it is of absolute necessity to know it, and believe it, and obey it.

And in all this I am not picturing a rare or imaginary inquirer. There are many persons in this state of anxiety, and many others who have passed through it unsatisfied, and have drifted into indifference. I speak, of course, of the multitudes of honest non-Catholics who have ceased to believe in the system in which they were reared because it failed to teach them securely how to save their souls, but who have not yet despaired of finding some more satisfactory authority in religion. They believe in God, and they love God, and they know, moreover, that God " in these days hath spoken to us by His Son," that, in short, He sent Him into this world to reveal the Christian religion; but what precisely are the contents of that which He has revealed, and how they may lay hold upon it in such wise as to save their souls—this is their difficulty. It is, in other words, the old question of Authority. Who is to be their Teacher and Guide in this the supremest of all concerns ? Who, at this distance of time from the earthly sojourn and atoning Death of our Incarnate Redeemer, who is to bring Him to us, and us to Him, that we may know Him and hear His words, and have the merits of His Precious Blood applied to our souls ?

Now it is with these people in my mind that I offer the following papers. I would fain hope that they may be not only of interest to Catholics, but also of some use in assisting anxious Protestants to settle definitely and finally the grand affair of their salvation. One thing is clear enough: as the years advance there is an ever-increasing number turning away in disappointment from the Protestant method of settling the question, for they have found its spokesmen to be " dumb dogs not able to bark, and shepherds who know no understanding " (Isa. lvi. 10, 11), whose " trumpet gives an uncertain sound " (1 Cor. xiv. 8), and who " have forsaken the fountain of living water, and have digged to themselves cisterns, broken cisterns that can hold no water " (Jer. ii. 13). And I am sure there are at least some who only require to understand the clear and unassailable grounds on which the Catholic Church bases her claim to speak with Divine Authority, and they will submit themselves to her teaching, and experience that " joy and peace in believing " which so many before them have, by the mercy of God, found within her embrace.

CHAPTER I

THE TRUE MEANING OF FAITH

LET us, then, begin at the beginning. In the first place, *Faith is necessary ;* on this all are agreed, for, according to St. Paul, we are " justified by faith." Luther termed this faith the " article of a standing or a falling Church "; and as for Catholics, their belief concerning it is determined by the Council of Trent, which called it (Sess. vi., c. 8) " the beginning of human salvation, the foundation and root of all justification." But here, unfortunately, our agreement ends, for with the question that necessarily follows, " What is Faith ?" we are at once plunged into controversy. Ask the average Protestant, and you will find that by faith he means trusting in Jesus Christ for salvation, believing that He shed His Blood upon the Cross and washed all His sins away, personally accepting Christ and His offered Redemption. " The principal acts of saving faith," says the " Confession of Faith " (chap. xiv.), " are accepting, receiving, and resting upon Christ alone for justification, sanctification, and eternal life, by virtue of the covenant of grace." Or, to quote the more familiar answer of the Shorter Catechism to the question (No. 86): " What is faith in Jesus Christ ? Faith in Jesus Christ is a saving grace whereby we receive and rest upon Him alone for salvation as He is offered to us in the Gospel."

According to this doctrine, when we have faith in Christ, Christ accepts us and looks upon us as " righteous " even though we are not really so. He " imputes His righteousness " to us; He covers over our sins with His merits, much as a fall of snow covers a mudheap. And so Luther taught: " God cannot see in us any sin, though we are full of sin; nay, are sin itself, inside and out, body and soul, from the top of the head to the soles of the feet, but He only sees the dear and precious Blood of His Beloved Son, our Lord Jesus Christ, wherewith we are sprinkled " (quoted in Verres, " Luther, an Historical Portrait," p. 139).

Now it must be said at once that this is not the true and proper and Scriptural meaning of faith at all. That the word may sometimes bear this meaning—trust in a person, belief in his power, hope and confidence—is certainly not to be denied. You find this kind of faith in such cases, for example, as St. Jas. i. 6, " Let him ask in faith, nothing wavering "; and St. Luke, viii. 48, " Daughter, thy faith hath made thee whole "; and St. Matt. xv. 28, " O woman, great is thy faith "; and even St. Matt. xiv. 31, " O thou of little faith, wherefore didst thou doubt ?" and in other passages. But what we deny is that this is the kind of faith Almighty God demands of us as necessary for salvation, *saving faith*, justifying faith. In fact, St. Paul himself actually distinguishes them, the one from the other, and represents the former—trust, assurance, confidence—to be an effect of the latter: " In whom we have boldness and access with *confidence*, by the *faith* of him " (Eph. iii. 12). Faith we hold to be " a supernatural gift of God, which enables us to believe without doubting whatever God has revealed " (Catechism, Q. 9); or, according to the fuller definition of the Vatican Council, " a supernatural virtue by which, through the grace of God inspiring and helping us, we believe as true all that God has revealed, not on account of their truth as perceived by natural reason, but on account of the authority of God revealing them, who can neither deceive nor be deceived." This is faith: an intellectual belief: the assent of the mind to certain truths; the acceptance of whatever doctrines God has taught, simply because He has taught them. It is not a mere " accept-ance of Christ," as Protestants assert, by an act of the will; though it is that, too, in the sense that we accept the doctrine that Christ died to atone for our sins. Cer-tainly the will must move the intellect to make this act; and again, grace is required to move the will to operate, as Our Lord taught when He said: " No man can come to Me except the Father, Who hath sent Me, draw him " (St. John vi. 44). In the long run, therefore, it is all a matter of God's mercy bestowing grace. " For by grace you are saved through faith, and that not of yourselves; for it is the gift of God " (Eph. ii. 8). But confining our-selves for the present to the *act of faith,* which is the effect of the *virtue of faith,* we say that, according to Catholic teaching, which is Scripture teaching, it is simply *an act of your intelligence ;* it is believing and accepting with your mind, assenting and consenting to whatever truths Almighty God has made known, however difficult or impossible they may seem, simply because He has revealed them. This, and nothing else, is true faith.

I could adduce many texts to prove this, but I shall quote only one, for I am writing not to *prove* the Catholic doctrine, but only to explain and illustrate it, so that from a general view of the whole Catholic system you may be led to see how reasonable and unassailable, how beautiful, satisfying, and consoling it is. " Go ye into the whole world," said Our Lord, " and preach the Gospel to every creature. He that believeth and is baptized shall be saved; but he that believeth not shall be condemned " (St. Mark xvi. 15, 16). Now, Our Lord is here speaking of *justifying* faith: " he that believeth shall be saved." And the faith He speaks of is to be that faith by which the Gospel is to be believed. And what is the Gospel ? It is the whole Christian religion, the whole scheme of salvation as announced by the Apostles in all its parts. " Go and teach all nations." " Preach the Gospel to every creature." Now, to believe that is an intellectual act, a work of the intelligence, accepting and assenting to the truths of the Gospel. It is not, as I said before, merely the fact of believing that Christ died for you upon the Cross, and trusting to that for salvation. That is only a part of God's Revelation. A man stands up in a meeting, and says he is " saved " because " God so loved the world as to give His only-begotten Son that whoso-ever believeth in Him may not perish but may have ever-lasting life," and " he that believeth in the Son hath ever-lasting life " (St. John iii. 16, 36), and " He loved me and gave Himself for me." Or he buttonholes his neighbour at an Evangelistic meeting, and asks him, " Are you trusting in the Blood ?" and " Have you decided for Christ ?" and if he gets an answer in the affirmative, he will say : " Hallelujah ! You are on the Lord's side ! You are saved !" I know all this, because I have seen it and heard it, and taken part in it. But that is not faith. It is a mere sentiment, a feeling, a persuasion—I am afraid more or less fanatical—concerning one single point of the Christian Revelation. It is narrowing faith down to one particular act in Our Lord's Redemption, and ignoring all the rest. From this description you would never imagine that Jesus Christ taught anything about the Church, or the Sacraments, or good works. It is therefore essentially and fundamentally a false notion of faith—a delusion and a heresy.

St. Paul has given us an inspired description of faith : " Faith is the substance of things to be hoped for [*i.e.*, the basis and foundation on which rest the blessings of salva-tion we hope for], the evidence of things that appear not [*i.e.*, the making certain for us things that are not visible to the senses, nor perceived by reason] " (Heb. xi. 1). This faith, by which " the just man lives " (Heb. x. 38), consists in a firm belief in the things revealed by God, as all the examples in this chapter (xi.) of the Epistle to the Hebrews clearly shows. It is an act of the intellect by which we recognize such truths of revelation, for instance, as the forming of the world by the Word of God (verse 6), and even the very existence of God as our future Judge (verse 3). It was belief in God's Word, howsoever made known to them—a belief formed in the mind and with the intelligence, and inspiring hope and confidence—which enabled Henoch and Noah and Abraham and the rest to do all those things for which they are praised by the sacred writer. They believed on the authority of God, Who made revelations and promises to them.

Such is the nature of that faith which is necessary for salvation in every part of Holy Scripture, and especially the New Testament. In the true sense, therefore, the Scriptural and the Catholic sense, we may define faith to be the willing and deliberate submission of the mind to revealed truth, the acceptance of and belief in all that God has revealed. And anything less than this is not faith.

CHAPTER II

FAITH NECESSARY FOR CHRISTIANITY

THE faith to which I have been referring is called a " *supernatural* gift of God "—partly, no doubt, because it is concerned with truths above the natural order, which our unassisted intelligence cannot comprehend, but principally because this faith must come from God Himself, and cannot be acquired in any other way. You have it not by nature; you cannot get it by seeking for it, either in books or in the world around you or anywhere else; it is a free, unmerited gift of God. And after sanctifying grace, it is undoubtedly the most precious gift God can bestow on man, because it enables him to believe the Gospel, and without it you cannot believe. Let me explain why. There are many things in the Christian religion—truths, dogmas, facts, call them what you will—that the natural man finds it hard, indeed impossible, to believe. Observe, I do not say impossible only to *understand*, but impossible even to *believe*.

Christianity is a supernatural religion; it is full of mysteries and miracles. The Christianity which Rationalists and Modernists in our day attempt to recommend—a religion stripped of mysteries and emptied of all supernatural elements—is not the Christianity of Jesus Christ, nor of the Bible, nor even of what is called " Orthodox Protestantism." We must either take Christianity with its mysteries or leave it alone, for the two stand or fall together. And this applies to Protestant as well as to Catholic. The religion of Jesus Christ asks him to believe not only what he never saw and what no one ever saw, but what no one ever can see, and what from the very nature of the case cannot be *proved* or accounted for on natural grounds in any way whatsoever. We have only to refer to the Apostles' Creed, which many Protestants profess as well as we. Take the doctrine that Our Lord was " conceived by the Holy Ghost," or the " forgiveness of sins," or the second coming of Christ, or " the life everlasting "; or, again, the existence and guardianship of angels, or the reality of Heaven and Hell. These are realities, but spiritual realities; you cannot see or touch or handle them; they are not proper subjects of natural science or reason; you must take them on faith, as *revealed* by God. And it is precisely these things which Rationalists, who walk by sight and not by faith, reject. " The sensual [natural, Authorized Version] man perceiveth not these things that are of the Spirit of God, for it is foolishness to him; and he cannot understand, because it is spiritually examined [discerned, Authorized Version]" (1 Cor. ii. 14).

Take, for example, the Doctrine of the Blessed Trinity— that in God there are three Persons, God the Father, God the Son, and God the Holy Ghost, and yet there are not three Gods, but one God; the three Divine Persons are all one and the same God. The natural intelligence instinctively rebels against this; there is nothing like it in the sphere of Nature as known to us—it is, in short, a *mystery*, that is, a truth which is above reason but revealed by God. If this doctrine came to us on merely human authority, we should certainly refuse to accept it.

Or, again, take the Incarnation—the doctrine that the Infinite and Eternal God was for a period carried within the womb of a woman, and that the little Infant lying in the manger of the stable at Bethlehem, poor and helpless, was none other than the Omnipotent Creator of Heaven and earth ! Or think of the Passion and Death of Jesus Christ. Could the mind of man, unaided by God, take it in that that Sufferer, scourged, kicked, mocked, spat upon, reviled, sold for a price, was really the Second Person of the Blessed Trinity ?—that the Man nailed to the Cross, and hanging between Heaven and earth, bleeding and agonizing, the butt and sport of a vile rabble, and executed as a rebel, an outcast, and a blasphemer, was yet the Good God who loved us with an everlasting love ?

Or, again, take the Blessed Sacrament : how could we ever believe that the small, round, White Thing which we call the Sacred Host, which has the appearance of bread, and which our senses—touch and taste and sight—tell us is bread, yet is *not* bread at all, but is the true Body and Blood of God the Son made Man, together with His soul and Divinity ?—that It is as really and truly Jesus Christ, God and Man, as was the Child in Blessed Mary's arms, or as the Saviour upon the Cross, or as the Redeemer at God's right hand in heaven ?   How could we believe that the Eternal God, " whom the Heaven of Heavens cannot contain," is yet confined within the tabernacle on the altar, enclosed within a small ciborium, or carried by a priest in a pocket-pyx ?   Once more : take the eternity of Heaven and the eternity of Hell ; our minds, *naturally*, cannot conceive it.   Or, lastly, take the Resurrection of the Body—the dogma that at the general judgment we shall rise again with the same bodies as we have now ; that, no matter whether you have been burned to ashes, or become food for the fishes, or been devoured by wild beasts, or been reduced to dust in the grave, yet your body will be raised again and joined to your soul, and in body and soul reunited you will be found either in Heaven or in Hell.   I repeat, that these and other doctrines of the Christian religion are simply incredible to a man without faith ; he would not and could not accept them ; and, what is more, to many they have appeared not only incredible, but unreasonable, unnecessary, and absurd.

But so soon as you have faith you believe them, and

have no difficulty in believing them. Faith is like a telescope. Astronomers tell us that on a clear night one
can see with the naked eye about three thousand stars.
But look through a powerful telescope, and you will see
many millions. They were in the heavens all the time,
but you could not discern them. So is it with the truths
of the Christian religion. Many of them seem hard,
difficult, impossible; faith comes, and at once you find
it easy to believe then. As an example of what I mean,
imagine two friends visiting a Catholic church—the one
a Catholic, the other a Protestant. So soon as they enter,
the Catholic drops on his knee and remains for a moment
or two in prayer; the other stands unmoved, gazes round
him, and wonders what the Catholic is doing. What
makes the difference in their mode of acting ? The difference is that one has faith, the other has not. By faith the
Catholic knows and believes that Our Blessed Lord is
present on the altar, and consequently he genuflects and
adores Him; the Protestant, without faith, neither knows
nor believes in Our Lord's Presence. The first has the
spiritual telescope, and discerns Our Divine Lord in the
tabernacle, though under the appearance of bread—

> " Faith for all defects supplying,
>   Where the feeble senses fail."—*Benediction Hymn.*

—the second, destitute of such an instrument, neither
knows, believes, nor recognizes Him. " There hath stood
One in the midst of you Whom you know not."

Or, again, take the Immaculate Conception—the doctrine that the Blessed Virgin Mary, by a singular privilege
of grace bestowed on her through the merits of her Divine
Son, was preserved free from the least guilt or stain of
original sin. The Catholic, of course, says: " I believe this,
I hold this, with all my heart and soul." The Protestant
says: " No, I do not believe it, and cannot see it." What
makes the difference here ? Again, faith. Faith has
given the one light, so that he sees the truth revealed by

God; the other, without the light of faith, can only look into the darkness. You might say the same in regard to many other Catholic doctrines—*e.g.*, Purgatory, Confession, Indulgences, Masses for the living and the dead, and the like. The Protestant rejects and denies them; the Catholic spontaneously accepts and rejoices in them. It all depends upon the presence or the absence of the great gift of faith. I was right, then, in saying that after grace it is the greatest of all gifts. When a man has it, he is able to accept without hesitation all the mysteries of Christianity, whether he understands them or not. The man who has it not cannot and will not believe them, any more than a bird can fly without wings, or a blind man see, or an astronomer without his telescope perceive the stars that are invisible to the naked eye.

One Grand Characteristic.

Now there is one grand characteristic about Faith which is as much a cause of astonishment to the non-Catholic as it is a source of consolation to the Catholic; I mean, of course, that it enables him to believe *without doubting*. There is not the shadow of a shade of doubt in the soul of a Catholic about any of the truths of religion. Where there is true faith, there is not, and there cannot be, any doubt. The two things are mutually exclusive, as if one should say, where there is light there is no darkness. Ask a Catholic: " Is there a Hell ? Is there an endless Hell ? Will people dying unsaved burn for ever ?" He will reply at once, without hesitation: " Yes, certainly." Ask a Protestant, and he will answer: " Well, I do not know for certain. Some say yes, and some say no." He has doubts, because he has not faith. Again, ask a Catholic: " Do you really believe there is a Purgatory ? Do you really believe the Blessed Virgin was conceived without sin ? Do you really believe the priest can forgive sin ? Do you really believe the Pope is infallible ? Do you really believe that the Sacred Host is the true Body and Blood of Jesus Christ ? Do you honestly believe these things without the faintest suspicion or doubt ?" The answer comes back, instantaneous and unfaltering: " I do, as firmly as I believe in my own existence."

Ask a Protestant, on the other hand, about some of the articles of his creed—and he will hesitate and shuffle. He may be disposed to believe them himself; but he knows that there are many good and learned men in his communion who hold a contrary belief, and his confidence is shaken, and he is driven to admit that there are differences of opinion about the matter, and that therefore one dare not be too dogmatic. In short, he is very much in the position of the woman at the well of Samaria, who was so puzzled in her conversation with Our Lord that she took refuge in the saying: " I know that the Messias cometh (who is called Christ); therefore, when He is come, He will tell us all things " (St. John iv. 25).

A Catholic might not be able to *understand* every article of his belief; he might not be capable of explaining it to others in a very intelligible or convincing manner; he might not be able to defend it in controversy—indeed, as a mere matter of polemics, he might easily be floored by the seemingly weighty objections of some acute and practised adversary. But nothing of this would for a moment shake his *faith* or alter his *belief*. To believe is one thing, to understand is another, and a hundred difficulties, as Cardinal Newman remarks, do not make one doubt. Hence it is that the imperfectly instructed Catholic, though vexed, harassed, struck dumb, and not improbably infuriated by the superior skill of the Protestant objector, nevertheless sticks to his belief through thick and thin, and concludes by saying: " Well, I cannot answer you; I cannot meet your arguments; but I know the doctrine is true as surely as I know that two and two make four, and I would gladly lay down my life for it."

You might, then, convince a Protestant that, in the light of modern thought and study, his most cherished beliefs were mistaken; but you could never so convince a Catholic. Ply him with objections and difficulties as you will, set a score of the most brilliant Modernists or Higher Critics or Rationalists or anti-Popery men to overwhelm him with their arguments—it is all to no purpose, you will never move him; he is as certain at the end as he was at the beginning that his beliefs are the Truth of God. Now, Protestants would probably consider this attitude one of sheer unreasoning obstinacy and mental obtuseness; and if it were a question of truth solely within the sphere of nature, it might deserve the name. But being within the sphere of religious and supernatural truth, Catholics call it not obstinacy but faith. Whence, then, comes this absolute impossibility of shaking a Catholic's faith, this entire absence of doubt ? It comes from the very nature of faith itself, which means *believing a truth on the authority of God*. The faith we are now speaking of is Divine, supernatural faith, in virtue of which a Catholic says, " I believe this and I believe that, because Almighty God Himself has said it, Who can neither deceive nor be deceived "; and in virtue of which St. Paul said: " I know in whom I have believed, and I am certain " (2 Tim. i. 12).

Now, as there are different kinds of faith we shall best understand what Divine faith is by first seeing what it is not.

CHAPTER III

HUMAN FAITH AND DIVINE FAITH

To begin with, then, Faith is not a mere *probability*, nor an *opinion*, nor even a *conviction*, for all these are liable to be reversed in the course of time; there is no absolute certainty implied in such states of the mind, for doubt or fear as to the opposite being true is not excluded. Now, what we are dealing with at present, and what we wish to have, is certainty which will exclude all doubt.

How, then, can I become certain about anything? Broadly speaking, I may arrive at certitude in two ways, (1) by Evidence, and (2) by Authority, or the testimony of another.

1. The certitude produced by Evidence may be of various kinds. There are, for example, self-evident truths, such as that the whole is greater than the part; the shortest distance between two given points is a straight line. These and the like propositions, axioms, or first principles, whatever you may call them, are so evidently and intrinsically true that the mind assents to them so soon as the terms which express them are understood. Again, I may arrive at certainty by the evidence of my own *senses*, my own *observation*, my own *experience*. I know, for example, that vinegar is bitter and sugar is sweet. I know that water will freeze with the thermometer standing at 32° F. I know that men can navigate the air. I know that a dose of strychnine will kill a dog. I know that a lighted match will set off gun-

powder. I know the law of gravitation. I am certain about all these and a thousand other things, for they are matters falling within my own knowledge; I have proved and tested them for myself. Such are matters of human knowledge or scientific certainty, which is concerned with natural truths, and is acquired by reason working upon evidence that a man can gather for himself. But for such facts as these no faith is required. When we speak of faith we come to a different cause or motive of certainty altogether.

2. Faith comes into play when I believe a truth, a statement, a doctrine on the Authority or testimony of another. Now there is Human Faith and there is Divine Faith, and the two must be carefully distinguished.

(1) Human Faith is exercised when I accept a statement on authority which is purely human, howsoever it may reach me, whether by speech or writing, or any other way. A man tells me something; I see no reason to doubt his word. I trust him, and I believe him; I accept the truth on his authority. For instance (to take one or two random illustrations), George Combe tells me in his book, " The Constitution of Man " (p. 12), that a certain kind of moss is abundant in Lapland in winter, and that the reindeer feeds on it. He tells me that the broad hoofs of camels qualify them to walk on sand, and that they have stomachs fitted to retain water for a considerable time, and hence are able to flourish amid arid tracts of sand where the reindeer would hardly live for a day. He tells me that the fly, walking or sleeping on the ceiling over my head, has a hollow in its foot from which it expels the air, and the pressure of the atmosphere on the outside of the foot holds it fast to the objects on which the inside is placed. Now I quite believe these statements of Combe. I accept them from such a reliable authority, though I have never verified them for myself. And therein I exercise a human faith. Again, I read in Professor

Arthur Thomson's work, " Darwinism and Human Life," that there are eighty species of a certain land-snail in the Bahama Islands; that in 1796 the speed of an English trotter was a mile in 2 minutes 37 seconds, whereas now it is a mile in 2 minutes 10 seconds; that the average American oyster has 16,000,000 eggs; that there exist quaint Japanese waltzing mice, which waltz round and round in circles; and that " the cholera bacillus can duplicate every twenty minutes, and might thus in one day become the number 5 with seven noughts after it, with the weight, according to the calculations of Cöhn, of about 7,366 tons." These interesting assertions also I am quite prepared to accept from such a distinguished scientist. I take his word for them. He is an honest man, with no object in deceiving me. His credentials, his titles to be believed, are beyond cavil.

No doubt it is true enough that the certainty arising from such faith will vary in degree and in intensity, according to the credibility of the witness—his scientific reputation, his veracity, and so on. And my certainty will be stronger and more immoveable if I know that his testimony is backed by many others of equal eminence. Faith in many witnesses tends to produce greater certainty than faith in one. The statement of many astronomers, for example, that the sun is 90,000,000 miles distant from the earth is more certainly true for me than the single assertion of one astronomer about the planet Mars, or of one biologist about the organism of some obscure plant or animal. The main point, however, is that here I am exercising human faith, accepting truths on the authority of man.

(2) Well, as St. John says (1 Ep. v. 9): " If we receive the testimony of men, the testimony of God is greater." And Divine faith simply means accepting the truths that *God* teaches us, not about science but about religion, and only *because* He teaches them: it is *believing something on Divine authority*. Surely this is reasonable enough ? If

I believe what a mere man tells me, surely I cannot refuse to believe what Almighty God tells me. If I assent without difficulty to the wonderful statements of scientists and astronomers about things which I have never studied myself, and of which I know absolutely nothing, merely because these clever and learned men make them, how can I hesitate about assenting to the teaching of Almighty God ?

OBJECTION ANSWERED.

Someone perhaps will here object: " But the truths of religion are so mysterious and so difficult, so far beyond our understanding, so impossible to verify or prove, that my intellect cannot accept them as easily as natural and scientific truths which are capable of being inquired into and demonstrated."   To this I have two replies to make:

1. In the first place, I answer that the very same objection applies to many of these latter truths.   Nature herself is full of mysteries.   Can you explain, for example, how a crop of corn springs up ?   The farmer traverses the field in spring, casting handfuls of seed hither and thither; in a few months the field is covered with beautiful yellow grain.   Can you explain the process that goes on underground ?   Did you ever see the operation by which the little seeds die and fructify, and then send up the waving stalks of corn ?   Can you explain how the tiny acorn, half the size of your thumb, springs up in a generation into an immense oak-tree ?   Can you unravel to me the origin of life itself ?   How an egg, for instance, which seems to contain only a yellow and white fluid, will, if placed under a hen in suitable conditions, send forth a live chicken in a short time ?   Better still, do you know, can you explain, how life springs up within the unborn child ?   Can you explain how the earth and all its riches were evolved out of chaos ?   You cannot explain these

things; no one can—they are mysteries of Nature.   Yet
you believe them, you accept them; you cannot help it.
You see them for yourself, and seeing is believing.   Well,
surely we are entitled to exercise a similar belief in regard
to the truths of religion, even though we do not understand them ?

2. Again, if we consider the matter properly we shall
see that Divine faith is much more reasonable than
human faith.   And why ?   Because there is always an
element of doubt in the credibility of man, but none in
that of God.   You can never be absolutely certain about
man's word: you are liable to be deceived by him; but
with Almighty God that is impossible.   He can " neither
deceive nor be deceived."   As St. Paul says: " God is
true, and every man a liar " (Rom. iii. 4).   And as Balaam
said: " God is not as a man that He should lie, nor as the
son of man, that He should be changed " (Num. xxiii. 19).
For example, a man tells me he has visited New Guinea,
and declares the Papuan women wear their hair trailing
on the ground.   Or he says that the blue hens in Australia
lay twice as many eggs as white ones; and that there are
green snakes in Egypt which sleep for five years without
food.   Now, the man may be speaking the truth, but,
on the other hand, he may not.   I have never been either
to Papua or Egypt or Australia, and I have nothing but
the man's word for these remarkable statements.   The
man may be in general trustworthy; still, on this occasion
he may be joking.   Perhaps he was never in these lands
at all; perhaps he is telling lies; perhaps he may only have
read about them; perhaps he has been misinformed or
imposed upon by someone else.   In short, there are
a dozen reasons that might make me hesitate before
accepting his story, and if I do accept it, I may find
in a short time that the story was very far from the
truth.

You object that this is an extreme case, that this is
reducing the whole thing to an absurdity.   Well, put the

matter at its best. Take statements made in sober earnest by a man of irreproachable veracity and seriousness; take statements vouched for by the cleverest and most learned men, by the most approved authorities; I still say there always lurks an element of uncertainty about them, a possibility at least of error. Are not the " conclusions " of the greatest men constantly being reversed, and their " facts " overturned ? This is no discredit to them; it is a necessity of their limitations. After all they are but human, and to be human is to be fallible.

But even supposing we have the most unimpeachable of human authority—and I admit that the testimony of competent witnesses can and does furnish the highest, even complete, human certainty—still it cannot be compared to that of Almighty God ! One is human, the other Divine. Here is the difference. " Why," asks the Catechism, " must we believe whatever God has revealed ?—We must believe whatever God has revealed because God is the very Truth, and can neither deceive nor be deceived." Notice the word " must." Not only *may* we, but we must believe what God teaches. That we safely *may* do so is plain enough to any intelligence. There is no possibility of God deceiving us. He cannot mislead or mock us in anything, least of all in matters concerning our eternal salvation. Nor can anyone mislead God. He is the Truth, as well as the Way and the Life. So that, whatever God teaches must, from the very attributes of the Divine character, be true. Hence we may, with a confidence born of absolute certainty, believe as true, and as necessarily true, whatever God is pleased to tell us.

And we not only may, but we *must* believe it—must, not, of course, through any physical compulsion or any external coercion whatsoever that takes away our freedom, but from a moral compulsion, in the sense that we must either believe or commit a sin.

So soon as we know that God has spoken, we are bound at once to say " I believe." To act otherwise would be rank rebellion and blasphemy. He is our Creator and our Lord and our Master; to refuse to believe His word would mean that the creature deliberately set himself up against his God.

CHAPTER IV

BEAUTY AND REWARD OF CATHOLIC FAITH

THIS, then, is the faith that Catholics have in matters of religion—Divine faith. We believe the truths of our most holy religion, not because we can prove them or have experienced them, not because we think them reasonable or beautiful or consoling (though they are all that)—these are all Protestant reasons for believing. We believe solely because Almighty God has taught us them. This is what theologians call the formal cause or motive of faith: the authority of God revealing. We have nothing whatsoever to do, in the first instance, with the intrinsic nature of the truths taught; nor does it matter whether they are hard or easy of belief, whether they seem probable or improbable; enough for us that Infinite Truth has revealed them. Doubtless we know that God could never teach anything that was not beautiful and reasonable, for all His works are perfect. Yet it is not for this that we assent to them. It is not for us to question why He should have taught this, or why He should have done that; God is not obliged to explain His words or to justify His acts.

One man says: " Why should Jesus Christ have instituted the Sacrament of Penance ? Could He not have arranged for the forgiveness of sins some other way ?" I answer, Jesus Christ has not been pleased to tell us; that is all. But the fact that He has instituted Confession remains all the same. Personally, I do not relish going to Confession, nor, so far as I know, does any Catholic;

and were it not necessary and obligatory, comparatively few, I should think, would ever approach it. But we believe in it because God has revealed it, and we practice it because God has commanded it.

Another man objects: "I cannot grasp the Real Presence. I do not see the need of It. Our Lord is in Heaven, and not upon earth. I cannot see how He can locate Himself in the small Host, or how He can be present in a thousand tabernacles at one moment." I answer again, and it is the only answer possible: "Your incapacity to understand these mysteries is no argument against their existence; and, what is more, it should be no bar to your believing in them if only your belief is grounded on the proper motive." We do not believe the truths of religion because we understand the why and the wherefore of them, or because they commend themselves to us by their reasonableness or suitability, but simply because God has taught us them. If He has made them known, there is no possibility of our calling them in question; whether we like them or not, whether we understand them or not, we must bow down and accept them without a word. We do not understand them in order that we may believe, but rather, according to the beautiful saying of St. Anselm: "We believe in order that we may understand" (credo ut intelligam).

Perhaps the best illustration of what I mean by real Catholic faith, and of the difference between Catholic faith and Protestant want of faith, is to be found in an incident recorded by St. John in the sixth chapter of his Gospel. After feeding the multitude with five loaves and two fishes, Our Lord fled to the mountain lest the people should take Him and make Him a King. Next day, however, they tracked Him out, and found Him at Capharnaum. They were thinking of the loaves they had got: Jesus wished to raise their thoughts up to the Bread of Life. "You were hungry yesterday," He said in effect, "and you were fed; to-day you are hungry again. You want more bread. Now, I will give you Bread, of which if you eat, you will never hunger any more. And the Bread that I will give is My Flesh for the life of the world." This announcement was the cause of immediate and deep dissension among His hearers. The Jews were the first to murmur, and said: " How can this man give us His flesh to eat ?" But Our Divine Lord repeated His doctrine more emphatically: " Except you eat the Flesh of the Son of Man and drink His Blood, you shall not have life in you." The Jews did not understand, and therefore did not accept it. Many of the disciples of Jesus then followed their example. " It is a hard saying," they said. " Who can hear it ?" And when rebuked by their Master for their unfaithfulness, they turned back and walked no more with Him (v. 62, 67). Here, then, we have two classes among His audience, who refused to believe what they could not understand and what they considered to be impossible.

Then it was that Our Blessed Lord turned to the Twelve and put their faith to the supreme test: " Will you also go away ?" Now notice: the Twelve did not *understand* their Master's saying about eating His Flesh and drinking His Blood any more than the others; they were mystified, unenlightened, awestruck—they did not pretend to understand. Yet they immediately *believed*. With a beautiful act of faith—with that childlike willingness so characteristic of Catholics, to believe whatever Almighty God tells them, no matter whether they understand it or not —they accepted the word of Jesus, they embraced the doctrine. And why ? Simply because Jesus, whom they acknowledged as their Lord, declared it. This was what we call, and rightly call, " blind faith." Simon Peter, answering for the Twelve, said: " Lord, to whom shall we go ? Thou hast the words of eternal life." Now, here surely is the touchstone of loyalty to Jesus Christ. On which side would Protestants have ranged themselves— with the Jews, or with the Twelve ? It hardly admits of a

3

doubt. They *are* on the side of the Jews and the faithless
disciples to-day, in regard to the Real Presence. " It is
a hard saying," they complain; " who can hear it ?"   And
yet they know, they must know if they read their New
Testament, that the doctrine came from the lips of the
Son of God.   If they have not faith, if they do not receive
the dogma on His authority now, how would they have
received it then ?

Here, then, is the voice of the true Catholic: " O my
God, I believe, not because I understand, but purely
because Thou hast said it."   And there are two or three
remarks I wish to make about this attitude of mind
before passing to the next point.

The Attitude of the Catholic Intellect.

1. In the first place, we see how truly *humble* is the
attitude of the Catholic intellect.   A man of real humility
acknowledges the weakness, imperfection, ignorance, and
darkness of his understanding.   He finds it easy and
natural to submit his intellect to the teaching of Almighty
God.   He would consider himself a fool beyond measure
if he, a poor, blind creature, were to limit the truths of
religion to those only which his own judgment approved
or comprehended.   A Catholic soul, then, is a humble
soul; he prostrates himself adoringly before his God, and
cries out : " O my God, I believe with all my heart whatever
Thou teachest me."

In the eyes of the world, no doubt, it is absurd to
believe what you cannot understand, but not so in the
eyes of God.   " Unless you be converted, and become
as little children, you shall not enter into the Kingdom of
Heaven."   A Catholic possesses this childlike faith.   A
child does not criticize, or dispute, or call in question, or
demand to know the reasons for everything that he is
taught; he accepts it without suspicion on the authority

of his teachers or his parents : for to the young mind these are virtually infallible. To us Almighty God is absolutely infallible; Him, then, we believe with the simplicity of little children. In so doing we are not afraid of being thought infantile, weak, slavish, unmanly. People who apply these epithets to us, as they do, neither know the nature of true faith nor possess it; and they are but pronouncing their own condemnation, according to the Scriptural standard. With our unhesitating, unquestioning, loving, adoring faith, like that of innocent children, we as Catholics are happy; and we know that it is immensely pleasing to God.

2. And how do we know this ? Because it *honours and glorifies Him* so much; it is the noblest testimony our intellect can pay to Him; it is the proof of our limitless faith in His veracity. To give an instantaneous " Credo," even when He announces the most stupendous and impenetrable mysteries, surely argues sublime trust in Him. " If some person," says Father St. Jure, S.J., in his beautiful " Treatise on the Knowledge and Love of Our Lord Jesus Christ " (vol. ii., chap. xx.), " asked me to believe for his sake that the sun is luminous, I do not think he would be greatly indebted to me for believing it, since my eyes deprive me of the power of doubting it; but if he wished me to believe that it is *not* luminous, I should testify great affection for him if, on his word, I admitted as true what my reason and will prove to be false; and I should give him the most signal tokens of the entire reliance I placed on his opinion, his judgment, the perfection of his sight. We therefore testify great love for God by believing simply, like children, all the mysteries of faith in which our reason is lost, and which our eyes not only see not, but often seem to see the contrary. Thus St. Paul says: ' Charity believeth all things.' "

We know, too, from Our Lord Himself how pleasing to Him is this simple faith. You remember the touching

incident on the apparition of the Risen Saviour to St.
Thomas, one of the Twelve (St. John xx. 24-29). Thomas
was not present when Our Lord appeared to the Apostles
the first Easter night; and when told by them " We have
seen the Lord," he refused to believe it, and declared:
" Unless I shall see and handle Him, I will not believe."
Hence he is called " the doubting Thomas." To satisfy
him Our Lord graciously condescended to appear before
him the following Sunday, and invited him, saying: " Put
in thy finger hither and see my hands, and bring hither
thy hand and put it into my side; and be not faithless
but believing." On this St. Thomas believed, saying:
" My Lord and my God !" " Jesus saith to him, Because
thou hast seen Me, Thomas, thou hast believed; blessed
are they that have not seen, and yet have believed." In
this sentence Our Lord pronounced a Divine eulogy on
an act of faith. To believe without seeing, without
proving—this is what pleases Him. For believing in his
Lord's Resurrection after seeing Him risen, Thomas
was deserving of no praise and no benediction, for he
could not help believing then. To have credited it before
proving it with his own eyes; to have assented to the word
of his fellow Apostles; in short, to have taken it on faith—
this would have won him praise and blessing. But he
missed the blessing because, before believing, he insisted
on having proof and demonstration. " Because thou
hast seen Me, thou hast believed."

3. And not only is there no blessing and praise, but
there is no *merit*, no credit, no reward for believing a
thing after you have proved and tested and tried it.
There is no merit, *e.g.*, in believing in the ebb and flow
of the tide, or in the law of gravitation, or in the existence
of flying machines, because we can prove the truth of
these things any day for ourselves; we know they are
facts from the evidence of our senses. In the same way
the angels and saints in Heaven are deserving of no reward and no merit for believing all the truths revealed

by God, because they see God face to face, and all truth in Him; they know it, as theologians say, intuitively; they are constrained to believe, as they are constrained to love. The Beatific Vision is itself their reward. There is no room for faith in Heaven: faith is changed to sight. But to believe the dogmas of religion which are not susceptible of being tested by the senses, and whose mysteries we cannot fathom; to believe unhesitatingly in the reality of persons and places and things we never saw and cannot prove by natural reason or evidence—this is something altogether different, something wonderful and sublime. It is worthy of all reward, because it is so contrary to our natural inclinations, and because it brings into play so much higher and nobler an act of man's intelligence. To believe, for example, with your whole heart and soul, in spite of all appearances to the contrary, that the Sacred Host is your Creator and your God under the species of bread, and that in Communion you receive God's Precious Body and Soul into your own body and soul; to believe that the Blessed Virgin was conceived without that guilt and stain of sin which has rested on every other human being that ever lived; to believe in the existence of souls in Purgatory, and that indulgences can be applied by the living to assist them— I say to believe all this, and much else in the Catholic Faith, needs faith—intense, profound, stupendous faith, in short, Divine faith—and nothing less. It is not an ordinary act of the intellect, it is extraordinary—indeed, supernatural—and only a Catholic is capable of it. He accepts these truths of Revelation because God has taught them to him, and for this reason only; and for that God will reward him. He is not compelled to believe them against his will, as he is compelled to believe mathematical truths. Twice two are four; the whole is greater than the part; you have no choice there; you must believe that: it is what we call a " geometrical necessity." But the Immaculate Conception, Purgatory, the Real Presence

—a man is free to reject them and take the consequences. Thousands and millions, as a matter of fact, have rejected them. In so doing they sin, more or less; in accepting them, you merit a reward exceeding great. " Blessed are they that have not seen and yet have believed."

CHAPTER V

PROTESTANT'S FAITH THROUGH THE BIBLE

LET us return now to the well-disposed Christian whom we pictured to ourselves as anxiously searching for the truth. Arrived at this point, he says: " I see now the necessity of faith and the true meaning of it. I see how reasonable it is. I am prepared to believe whatever Almighty God has revealed, no matter how dark and mysterious it may seem. But the difficulty with me now is, how am I to know what God has revealed ? Where am I to find it ? Who will unfold it to me ?" Now here undoubtedly is the crux of the whole question, the key of the situation. It involves the tremendous controversy about authority in religion. To answer this question is to answer the question, " What is the Rule of Faith ?" and the answer will depend upon whether he who makes it is Catholic or Protestant. Even among Protestants the answers will vary. Some, like the Rationalists, will claim Reason alone as their ultimate authority, admitting no religious truth but such as they can prove and understand. Others, like the Agnostics, will accept neither religion nor faith, and declare they can never be sure of knowing anything at all. But none of these systems would satisfy our inquirer, who professes to be a Christian acknowledging a supernatural Revelation; we need not, therefore, stop to discuss them. The only other possible answer from the non-Catholic side to the question " How am I to know what God has revealed ?" is that which the vast majority of non-Catholics would offer—viz., " By the Bible. The Bible is the sole Rule of Faith. God has revealed all truth through the Bible. It is the Word of God, and what is not there, is not the Word of God."

Now, I do not intend, for the limits of space would not allow me, to prove at length the impossibility of the Bible as the rule of faith; that would involve a separate treatise by itself, and this can be found in many books, great and small, that deal specially with the subject. (On this question, I may, perhaps, be allowed to refer to " Where we got the Bible "—Sands and Co., 6d.)

My purpose in these pages is rather to explain the Catholic position regarding authority in religion, to show how simple, logical, and reasonable it is, and withal, how satisfying to the intellect, comforting to the soul, and most conformable to Holy Scripture itself. Nevertheless, I do not think it will be altogether useless if I devote at least one chapter to setting forth some plain and simple reasons why the Bible cannot of itself afford that certainty and completeness in matters of faith which every Christian desires to have.

Protestants, then, claim to go by the Bible and the Bible only; to take their religion from neither Church nor Pope, but from Holy Scripture alone. Let us grant that, for the present. As a matter of fact, they do not. They accept some things which are not in the Bible, and reject other things which are in the Bible. But that is a separate question altogether. I am dealing now only with what they profess to do; and it is a fact that they profess to take the Bible alone as their Rule of Faith. That Presbyterians and Nonconformists profess this, everybody knows; but for Anglicans, too, in the last resort, the supreme deciding authority is the Bible. Some people might say that their supreme authority is the Privy Council, but Anglicans object to this, and the Thirty-Nine Articles certainly name the Holy Scriptures as supreme. Article VI., for example, on " The Sufficiency of the Holy Scriptures for Salvation," begins in this manner: " Holy Scripture containeth all things necessary to salvation, so that whatever is not read therein, nor may be proved thereby, is not to be required of any man, that it should be believed as an article of the Faith, or be thought requisite or necessary to salvation." And Article XXI., on "The Authority of General Councils," says that "things ordained by them as necessary to salvation have neither strength nor authority, unless it may be declared that they be taken out of Holy Scripture."

The supreme authority for Catholics, on the other hand, is the living voice of the Catholic Church, speaking through the Pope or a General Council, and determining for us, with infallible assurance, what was the teaching of Jesus Christ and His Apostles, as found in Holy Scripture, and in Divine and Apostolic Tradition. For both Catholic and Protestant, then, we may say, the authority in religion is the Word of God; but with this fundamental difference—a difference, indeed, so fundamental that it really constitutes two quite separate authorities: for the Protestant the "Word of God" means only the written Word, the Bible; whilst for the Catholic the Word of God is the Word both written and unwritten—that is, the Bible plus Tradition. For the Protestant, again, the supreme interpreter of the Word of God is the reader himself; whilst for the Catholic the supreme interpreter is the Catholic Church, to whom alone it belongs to judge of the meaning both of Scripture and Tradition. I shall endeavour to show, as briefly as possible, how the Protestant system does not, and cannot, work. I shall try to demonstrate, in other words, the utter insufficiency of the Bible, taken alone, as a rule of faith. in the hope that any Protestant with a logical mind who may chance to see these pages, and wishes to have unassailable grounds for his belief and an impregnable rock for his faith, may be led by the grace of God to see that the Bible, apart from the Church, will not, and cannot, stand.

WHICH IS THE RIGHT BIBLE ?

1. In the first place, without the Church you cannot tell which is the right Bible. Many Bibles have appeared, especially since the invention of printing, differing both in size and doctrine. Everybody who has looked through a Catalogue of Bibles—say in the British Museum—knows this much. You do not know which of them all is true, which is complete, which is correct. Out of all the writings—and they were many—that were in circulation and in use in the Church in Apostolic and sub-Apostolic days, and that claimed to be genuine, you do not know which should be included in the Bible, and which should be excluded from it. You certainly cannot prove that your Bible contains precisely the inspired Word of God, no more and no less. You do not even know whether it is a correct version in English of the original languages— Hebrew and Greek—in which the Old Testament and New Testament respectively were first penned, or of the Aramaic language in which Our Blessed Lord spoke. A famous book now lies before me, " Errata of the Protestant Bible," by Thomas Ward, Esq., in which that learned gentleman, so long ago as the seventeenth century, enumerates I know not how many hundreds of errors— corruptions, mistranslations, falsifications, and omissions —of which the English translators had even then been guilty, in their various versions of the original text. And " what avails it," he very justly asks, " for a Christian to believe that Scripture is the Word of God, if he be uncertain which copy and translation is true ?" But you have neither the time nor the inclination, the scholarship nor the brains to undertake such an inquiry; and it would be evidently absurd to suppose that Almighty God required you to do it. For all this you must of necessity depend upon some higher authority.

The Catholic Church Compiled the Bible.

Now, it was the Catholic Church, in point of fact, away back in the fourth century, that settled what exactly the Bible was to contain and what it was to omit. She settled that by the decrees of her Councils—notably, those at Rome, Hippo, and Carthage, and by the decisions of her Popes, especially Gelasius, St. Damasas, and St. Innocent I. They separated the wheat from the chaff, the true from the false, the genuine from the spurious, the inspired from the uninspired; their judgment was accepted by universal Christendom for a thousand years, and is so accepted to-day; and thus it is to the Catholic Church the Protestant owes the Bible that he has, incomplete though it be. For, although he has rejected a certain number of the books admitted into the Canon by the Church of the fourth and fifth centuries, now forming part of the Catholic Bible, it still remains true that all the books found in his Bible to-day were first examined and accepted by the Catholic Church of that age. They all passed her censorship, so to speak, and were declared to be apostolic and inspired. Without the Church's authority, therefore, and her venerable seal of approbation, you could not possibly define what the contents of the Bible should be. You might, indeed, compile a volume of Scripture according to your own notions, as many Protestants have done, producing Bibles of varying sizes and contents; you might include in such a collection some works of the great poets, as other Protestants seem anxious to do; but after all, you would have no guarantee that it was the Bible Almighty God intended, and that is the main thing.

What the Bible says of Itself.

2. Then in the next place, the Bible was never meant to be, and nowhere claims to be, the sole organ of God's Revelation, the sole depository of His revealed truth. There is not a single text nor any command of God to that effect. On the other hand, there are texts to prove that the writers of the New Testament themselves taught the necessity of listening to the voice of Tradition (the unwritten Word of God) as well as to that of the Sacred Scriptures (the written Word); they could not have conceived of a Christian doing anything else. For instance, only a part of Our Lord's words and deeds is reported in the Holy Gospels. St. John says (xxi. 25): "There are many other things which Jesus did, which, if they were written, everyone, the world itself, I think, would not be able to contain the books that should be written." St. Paul, writing to his Thessalonian converts, bids them "hold the traditions which you have learned, whether by word or by our Epistle " (2 Thess. ii. 14). The Apostle, it will be observed, here places on one and the same level of authority all inspired teaching, whether it be committed to writing or conveyed only by word of mouth. The same remark applies to that other injunction of his, to St. Timothy (2 Tim. ii. 2): " The things which thou hast heard of me by many witnesses, the same commend to faithful men who shall be fit to teach others also." Where are all these traditions—apostolic and Divine traditions, not the mere " word of man " Protestants are so fond of reproaching us with, but the *Word of God handed down orally*—where are all those Divine words concerning " the Kingdom of God " that Our Lord spoke during the forty days between His Resurrection and His Ascension (Acts i. 3) ? They were the complement of the written Word; they were not, and could not be, lost; they were transmitted with the same veneration as were

the Holy Scriptures from one generation to another; that is certain. But it is equally certain that they are repudiated by Protestantism.

To continue, then, I say that an honest pagan, or unprejudiced outsider of any kind, would never come to the conclusion, from a calm reading of the Bible, that it sets itself up as an exhaustive and exclusive statement of all truths revealed by God, and he would never find God appealing to it as such. He would not even discover Holy Scripture anywhere making any claim for itself to be inspired. The words of St. Paul to St. Timothy (2 Tim. iii. 16) commonly relied upon to prove this latter claim—" all Scripture is given by inspiration of God, and is profitable," as King James's version has it; or " every Scripture inspired of God is also profitable," as the Revised Version more correctly has it—these words, I say, are wholly inept as regards the New Testament, for they refer to the Scriptures of the Old Testament; and even so, they tell nothing against Tradition, and give us no information whatsoever as to which books are inspired Scripture, and which are not.

The Bible not its own Guarantee.

3. But further, even supposing the Scriptures did claim for themselves to be inspired, that of itself could never satisfy us. The Bible cannot possibly be its own witness, its own guarantee. *Every document must be authenticated and certified as correct by some authority extrinsic to itself.* This is common sense, and it is universally admitted. If a book is put into my hands claiming to be a Revelation from God—" The Flying Roll," for example, is often offered to people as such— I must have some satisfactory proof that it is a Revelation; that it is genuine, that it is what it claims to be. No prudent or sensible man would be satisfied with the

claims of the book itself. Or if I receive a document pur-
porting to contain some provisions of great importance
or benefit to me, I must have it guaranteed and authenticated by irrefragable evidence. I must have proof that
it is not a mere sham or imposture; its own unsupported
claims would never be considered in themselves decisive.
If I demanded before a judge that its provisions should
be carried out on my behalf without any proof, I should
be at once, and very properly, laughed out of court.

We all know there have been many sects, even in
modern times, that pretended to possess new Revelations
made by God. Why not admit all these as genuine and
Divine? You answer: " I must first have some proof,
some authority, that they are Divine, and this is wanting."
I reply that is precisely the Catholic contention about the
Bible. I must first have evidence, testimony, guarantee,
credentials, call it what you will, *external to the Bible* itself,
to assure me that it really is the inspired Word of God,
that the New Testament really is the authentic and
genuine work of the Apostles and Evangelists of Jesus
Christ. And such there is none, except the tradition
and authority of the Catholic Church. It was this that
made St. Augustine, as early as the fifth century, declare,
in the ever-memorable words: " I would not believe the
Gospel if the authority of the Catholic Church did not
oblige me to believe it "—" Ego vero Evangelio non
crederem nisi me Catholicæ Ecclesiæ commoveret auctori-
tas " (" Contra. Ep. Fund." v. 6).

CHAPTER VI

PROTESTANT THEORY FURTHER EXAMINED

But there are further reasons why the Protestant theory breaks down when carefully examined.

4. The Bible could not possibly be the sole organ of God's Revelation in times when it did not yet exist *as a Bible*. The various books of which it is composed were not written all at one time, but arose gradually; and confining ourselves for the moment to the New Testament, we know that all its books did not exist, even as separate and independent units, till at least 90 A.D.; for it was not till then, and some would say not until much later, that the last of its books, the Gospel of St. John, was written. And, what is more important still, it was not till three hundred years after that date that its scattered parts were gathered into one volume to form what is called the Canon of the New Testament. This is an historical fact which anyone may find recorded in the most elementary textbook, whether Protestant or Catholic, on the formation of the Canon. How, then, I ask, could the generations that passed away during that long period take for their Rule of Faith a Bible the whole of which they did not and could not know ? Why, it was not even definitively settled during all that time what Christian writings should go into the Bible and what should be kept out; what were inspired and Apostolic and what were not. For it is another fact of history that there were many Gospels and Acts and Epistles and Apocalypses circulating among Christian communities and claiming Apostolic authorship—some of them, like

the " Shepherd of Hermas " and the " Epistle of Barnabas," very popular; and others, like the " Epistle of St. Clement," actually read aloud as Scripture in church—which were nevertheless afterwards discovered and pronounced to be either not inspired or not Apostolic.   On the other hand, it is an equally certain historical fact that at the same period—that is, before the beginning of the fifth century—some of the genuine works of Apostles, such as the Epistle to the Hebrews, the second Epistle of St. Peter, and others, were called in question, disputed, and suspected, and had a fight to win admission into the Canon—a position accorded them at last by the decisive judgment of Popes and Councils, as has been already said.   At an epoch, then, of such uncertainty and conflict—I have no wish to exaggerate it, but that such uncertainty did exist no one dreams of denying—how was a man to find security regarding the truths revealed by Jesus Christ if he depended upon these writings alone ? It was a sheer impossibility; and the simple fact of the matter is, that Christians then did not form their beliefs in that way at all.   They learned the truths of salvation as Catholics and all those evangelized by Catholics learn them to-day, from the living voice of the teachers and missionaries whom the Catholic Church sent out with Divine authority, saying: " Go and teach all nations." Our Lord Himself wrote nothing of the New Testament; neither did He say to His Apostles, " Go and write," " Go and read to them," or " Go and give them the Bible."   Indeed, we may say that the idea of writing books to be afterwards collected into a volume of sacred Scripture was the very last thing the Apostles would ever dream of; such a notion would simply never enter their heads.   But Our Lord did say to them: " Go and preach the Gospel to every creature.   As my Father hath sent Me, even so send I you.   He that heareth you heareth Me.   I am with you always, even to the consummation of the world."   He constituted them, in other words, and in them their successors, a teaching Church to the end of time. Thus the history of the New Testament itself, and its own words, bear witness against the erroneous conception of Protestants regarding its place in God's economy for the salvation of mankind.

5. Once more, the Bible was literally inaccessible to the vast majority of Christians (not to speak of non-Christians) for a thousand years (roughly speaking) after it was completely formed, because the art of printing had not been discovered. A copy might, indeed, have been purchased, but only by the very rich. Is it conceivable that Almighty God, who desires that all men should come to the knowledge of the truth, should for so many centuries have left His people destitute of an adequate means of arriving at it? The Protestant thinks of Bible Societies flooding the country with the Scriptures at the present day, and says a man can go round the first corner and buy a New Testament for a few coppers. But let him for a moment think himself back to the days before the printing press, and what has he to say? In fact, for a considerable period after the first Bible was printed, which was in 1456, it was utterly beyond the power of the average Christian to possess himself of such an expensive volume; the Book had to be chained to a pillar in the church that people might have a look at it. The people, indeed, were made acquainted with the truths of the Christian Faith; but, again, it was in the Catholic way, the way that God intended—through His living and teaching organ, the Catholic Church, which explained and interpreted Holy Scripture for them. This was the primary authority, the pure fountain-head from which the people derived their knowledge of Christianity and of the means whereby they were to save their souls. Those who could read, and who did read the Bible as they had opportunity, read it for edification, meditation, comfort, spiritual support; they were Christians already, instructed in the Faith, and only

4

found in it what they had been already taught. A pre-Reformation Christian would have stared in astonishment if you had suggested any departure from this, the normal, God-appointed method of learning whatsoever He had revealed—just as he would have stared in astonishment if you had mentioned such things as Anglicanism or Presbyterianism, or Congregationalism. This is a new thing upon the earth, he would have said: "We have no such custom, nor the Church of God" (1 Cor. xi. 16).

6. And this leads us in the same line of argument to ask the question: "Even to-day, how can the Bible be the guide to God's Revelation for those who cannot read it—the illiterate, for example, the feeble-minded, and children?" I receive the answer: "They are taught by others who can read and explain it to them." Quite so, but that is doing the very thing that Protestants complain of in us—introducing a third party between God and the sinner; it impugns the self-sufficiency of Holy Scripture. The Protestant contention is that the sinner and the Bible can settle the affair of salvation between them; and I am pointing out certain classes of sinners who cannot so settle it. Here, at all events, Protestants are driven to confess that a teacher of some kind is an absolute necessity. And this of itself is an admission that the Bible, alone and apart, is not a complete and all-sufficient guide for all, whatever their age and condition; and if it is not that, it cannot be the guide designed by Almighty God. Moreover, the very fact of their resorting to Catechisms, and Formularies, and Creeds, and Confessions of Faith, and Articles of Religion, is another proof of the same thing. In strict consistency the only logical Protestants would appear to be the Quakers, who dispense with all such standards and depend entirely upon the "Inward Light."

THE BIBLE DIFFICULT AND OBSCURE.

7. And besides all this, the Book itself is far too difficult to serve as a guide without some competent authority to explain it. St. Augustine declared the things in the Scriptures he could not understand were more than those he could understand. St. Peter himself (2 Pet. iii. 16), writing of the things in St. Paul's Epistles "hard to be understood," admits that the "unlearned and unstable wrest the Scriptures to their own destruction." And no wonder, for the Bible necessarily deals with the profoundest mysteries and the deepest problems imaginable, those, namely, of Religion. A guide-book should be easy, simple, and clear. The Protestant says the Bible is the guide-book to Heaven. Well, I ask, is it simple, easy, and clear? Quite the reverse; everybody knows that it has been the most potent cause of controversy and the most fertile source of disagreement that ever existed. But that is not the fault of the Bible itself; the fault is in those who have misused it by putting it to serve a purpose for which it was never intended. It is full of difficulties and dark sayings, and even seems to reveal inconsistencies and self-contradictions to the man whose only key to its mysteries is his own private judgment. The Protestant says it is self-evident, it is quite clear what the Bible means, when the Holy Ghost guides you to the understanding of it. If that is so, then I ask, how is it that we have hundreds of warring sects all springing from the Bible—sects opposed to each other on every single doctrine, even the most fundamental, and yet all claiming the support of the Bible? Has the Holy Ghost guided each one to a different conclusion? To say so were flat blasphemy. One thing is certain: the Holy Ghost cannot teach yea and nay at the same time; He cannot teach one man one truth and another man its opposite. The sects, then, owe their origin, not at all to the inspiration

of the Holy Ghost, but to their own abuse of God's Word. Is the Bible, then, quite so simple and intelligible a guide after all ?

The truth is, you can make the Bible prove anything you like. There never was a crank, fanatic, impostor, or heresiarch yet that played upon people's ignorance for ever so short a time who did not twist and force the Sacred Scriptures to suit himself.

PROTESTANTS LEAN ON AUTHORITY.

8. But in reality the Protestants' claim to rest upon the Bible only for their doctrines is not genuine; what they do take, as a simple matter of fact, for their guide is not the Bible only without note or comment or other human interference, but the Bible interpreted by their own founders. A Presbyterian, *e.g.*, reads his Bible with the Calvinistic interpretation already in his mind. An Anglican comes to it with Anglicanism in his mind; the Lutheran with Lutheranism in his mind, and so with all the rest. They have learned their system of theology, and worship, and church government from their cate-chisms, their teachers, their parents, their clergy; and imbued with this, they come to the Bible, and, of course, they find all these things in it. What more natural ? They have been taught to find them there. In other words, they first learn Christianity, or at least a particular form of Christianity, on the authority of others, and then they have no difficulty in making the Bible square with it, and it with the Bible.

As a proof of this, let anyone put a Bible, without annotations, into the hands of any intelligent and un-prejudiced Pagan who had never heard of the various religious bodies that claim to be based upon it; will any one seriously assert that the Pagan would discover Presbyterianism there, or Anglicanism, or Lutheranism ?

I trow not. If you asked him, as St. Philip asked the Ethiopian eunuch, " Thinkest thou that thou understandest what thou readest ?" he would probably make the same reply as the eunuch: " How can I, unless some man shew me ?" Your answer to me, of course, is: " If he did not discover the Protestant system in the Bible, he certainly would not discover the Catholic system either." I rejoin at once: " We should not expect him to do so, without the aid of tradition." Nevertheless, I think he would be likely to find much more of Catholicism in it than of any other religion. But granting he would fail to find it, that only proves the very point that I am labouring to establish—viz., that the Bible by itself is far from being a clear and easy guide to Christian doctrine, and that it supplies Protestants with their theology only in so far as it is first interpreted and explained to them by their official teachers.

MODERN UNDERMINING OF THE BIBLE.

9. And if this was always true, even in ages when everyone believed every word of Holy Scripture, it is tenfold more true to-day. Who can fail to see how utterly impossible it has become to regard the Bible as the sole reliable channel of God's revelation in these days when its Divine authority is impugned, the authenticity and authorship of its books attacked on all sides, the genuineness of many passages of the sacred text disputed, and its inspiration and inerrancy treated as relics of a credulous age long gone by ? No Protestant, unless he be deliberately blind to the religious change that has taken place, can fail to see that, owing to the assaults of critics the most acute, and the researches of scholars the most profound all over the world, the Bible has lost its old position of authority for him. He cannot trust it in the same way; he does not know, in short, where he stands.

Let anyone read such a work as " Doctrine and Doctrinal Disruption," by Mr. W. H. Mallock—an independent thinker, with no interest in defending any creed in particular—and he will be convinced at once how foolish it would be in these days to build upon the Bible as on a foundation that could not be moved.

I should like, before closing this part of the subject, to quote a few sentences very much to our purpose from the work of a writer whose authority may have weight with some of my readers, Dr. Adolph Harnack, Professor of Church History in the University of Berlin. The book (now translated into English in the Crown Theological Library) is entitled " Bible Reading in the Early Church," and was written to advocate a theory of Harnack's which is far from favourable to the Catholic position. But throughout the volume the author, who is, I suppose, the most distinguished Protestant theologian in Germany, if not in Europe, makes some admissions which go far to support the foregoing contentions. He says, for example (pp. 12-13), referring to the famous controversy which Lessing had in the eighteenth century with the German patristic scholar Walch, and the German Protestant pastor Goeze: " Christian faith and a Christian Church existed before ever there was a New Testament. Lessing did not, indeed, discover this historical fact, but he first recognized its decisive importance, and with the power of genius established it as current truth. Never has a simpler incident had a grander result. From this time dates the gradual dissolution of orthodox Protestantism." And, again, speaking of " Lessing's fundamental thought, that the Rule of Faith is more ancient than the New Testament, and that the Church at first developed and grew without the New Testament," he says: " The thought itself is historically correct, and has shattered the tyranny of ancient Protestant dogma." Once more he speaks (p. 145) of " the undying service he (Lessing) has rendered, . . . in that he perceived that the New

Testament as a book and as the recognized fundamental document of the Christian religion originated in the Church." Thus far Harnack clearly perceives that the Bible was later than the Church, and arose from within it. But of even greater importance for our present argument is a passage in a note (p. 9) in which the Professor states as correctly as any Catholic could do the absolute necessity of an *authorized interpreter of Holy Scripture* : " An inspired document," he says, " is not only untranslatable without the same Divine assistance that created it, but it is also uninterpretable. Catholicism is, therefore, absolutely in the right in its claim that the power of interpreting Holy Scripture lies only in the Church, which alone has the promise to be led by the Holy Spirit into all truth. Inspiration and a sacred court of interpretation necessarily hang together. If Protestantism substitutes the endowment of each individual Christian with the Holy Spirit, this expedient is unsatisfactory, for the very reason that no provision is made for the case, which again and again recurs with each passage of Scripture, that the interpretations are divergent."

Now, Harnack has here surely put his finger upon the one grand flaw which, were there no other, would of itself be sufficient to condemn the Protestant theory of the exclusive authority of the Scriptures—the fact, namely, that the theory, when put in practice, leads people equally sincere to the most contradictory conclusions. Some say there are Three Persons in God, others One. Some believe that Jesus Christ was God, others that He was a mere man; some admit His Resurrection and miracles, others deny them. Some say there is a Hell, and an everlasting Hell; others say there is none, or at most a temporary one. Some believe in Infant Baptism, others reject it. Some believe in Baptismal Regeneration, others deny it. Some believe in the Real Presence of Our Lord in the Holy Eucharist, others in the Real Absence. The Lutherans, and Zwinglians, and Presbyterians, and

Anglicans have each a different theory about it. There have been endless dissensions about the Bible itself—its inspiration and its teaching. Differences about doctrine have been as widespread and as serious as those about Church worship, discipline, and government. In fact, there is not a single doctrine of Christianity, even the most solemn and awful, over which Protestants have not split and wrangled, setting up Church against Church, and pulpit against pulpit, and refusing in consequence even to sit down together at the Table of the Lord. There is no unity, only chaos. There is at least one sect for every day of the year. They cannot all be right; but each sect thinks it is right; so that it comes to this—that there is no such thing as absolute Christian Truth excluding error, but the truth is what each one thinks to be the truth. But this is not the Christianity of Christ, Who prayed " that they all may be one "; nor the Christianity of St. Paul, who said (Gal. i. 8): " Though we, or an angel from heaven, preach a Gospel to you besides that which we have preached to you, let him be anathema. As we said before, so now I say again, if anyone preach to you a Gospel besides that which you have received, let him be anathema." And hence, again, the question forces itself upon the mind of any thinking man: Is it conceivable that a system which results in such a scandal, such a shipwreck of Christian truth, and such a bewilderment of souls, could ever have been designed by a merciful Saviour to bring all men, learned and simple alike, " out of darkness into light," to unite them in " one body " and " one faith," to make them " of one mind in the Lord," and to " have peace " ?

You tell me that in spite of all criticism tens of thousands of sincere Christians still hold on to the Bible as the anchor of their soul. True, but they are few compared to the tens of thousands who have abandoned, and are abandoning, it. You will always find a large number of people who for one reason or another continue to cling to the creed they have inherited, no matter what it is, and in spite of all that may be said against it; and one reason is because, like the ostrich that buries its head in the sand, they refuse to look the danger in the face and flatter themselves that all is well.   But, on the other hand, there are, as I have said, multitudes of enquiring, discerning, thoughtful Protestants (and to these I would chiefly appeal) who have lost faith in the Bible because they are persuaded beyond all doubt, from what they have read and heard, that taken by itself it cannot be relied upon as a sure and certain guide to what God has revealed.   They know neither what the Bible is, nor which is the right Bible; nor what it means and teaches; nor which parts of it are safe; nor yet what is the true interpretation out of a dozen interpretations of many a passage of the most awful import; and they are crying out, " Who will show me the Teacher sent from God, that can speak to me with infallible authority, and can satisfy my troubled soul with the truth, and nothing but the truth, Almighty God wills me to believe ?"

CHAPTER VII

FAITH THROUGH AN INFALLIBLE CHURCH

THE Catholic here comes forward with his answer—an answer which, as I already hinted, settles for ever the tremendous question of authority in religion. It is No. 11 in the Penny Catechism: " I am to know what God has revealed by the testimony, teaching, and authority of the Catholic Church." And to the further question, " Who gave the Catholic Church Divine authority to teach ?" we have the answer: " Jesus Christ gave the Catholic Church Divine authority to teach when He said: Go ye and teach all nations." Here, then, is the organ and mouthpiece of God's revelation to men. All you have to do, if you wish to believe what God wishes you to believe, is to listen to the Living Voice of the Catholic Church, and accept her teaching. Granting that you admit the necessity of faith, and that you are willing to exercise it— that you are willing to believe whatever God teaches you— here is the way to exercise it: Believe whatsoever the Holy Catholic Church believes and teaches; be prepared to accept without doubting whatsoever she may in the future propose for your belief. You are not to search in the world of Nature to find out God; nor to hunt up books and ransack libraries; nor to go to clever scientists or learned philosophers; nor to inquire of any and every man that professes to know the Gospel; nor to run hither and thither through all the various sects; nor yet to run through the Bible itself, in search of God's truth. That is not the proper way at all; it is only wasting time. There is a far simpler and surer method than any of these

—the only true method, because the method of God's own appointing, and that is, to hearken, like a little child, to the voice of your holy mother the Catholic Church, and "receive with meekness the ingrafted word which is able to save your soul" (St. Jas. i. 21).

I have said this is God's method: I shall now proceed to prove it. 1. We start with this, that Jesus Christ was God the Son made man for us. He came down to redeem us from sin and Hell and to teach us the way to Heaven. The purpose of His Incarnation was that He might give Himself a sacrifice for sin, show us the example of a perfect life, reveal to us God's Holy Will, and teach us all necessary truth. Now, He came that all might be saved; hence He intended that His Divine Revelation should be known not only to His contemporaries, but to all generations that should ever live on earth until the last day: what plan would He take to secure this end? What method would He adopt to make it at least possible that the Gospel should be faithfully transmitted all down the ages?

That Almighty God, in His infinite wisdom and power, might have chosen diverse methods, is, of course, admitted: but the question is, in the present order of things, what method as a matter of fact did He choose? The Catholic Church gives the answer.

2. Jesus Christ, Incarnate God, began by choosing twelve men as His companions (St. Matt. x.), who are commonly called the Twelve Apostles. He trained them for three years, and fitted them for the great office He intended them to fulfil. He made Simon Peter their Leader and Chief. " Thou art Peter," He said to him, " and upon this rock I will build My Church, and the gates of hell shall not prevail against it. And to thee I will give the keys of the Kingdom of Heaven " (St. Matt. xvi. 18, 19; also St. Luke xxii. 32; St. John xxi. 15-17.) To these men, forming the Apostolic College, He committed His Gospel; them He selected as the depositaries of His

Heavenly Revelation; hence we call the truth Christ taught the Apostolic Deposit, or "the faith once delivered to the saints" (St. Jude 3). To the crowd at large, it is true, and to other followers, He preached and expounded the Gospel of the Kingdom; but the Twelve He instructed more fully and enlightened in a more intimate manner, and to them He taught and explained mysteries that were not made known at first to others (St. Matt. xiii. 11-13, 16-17). All who believed in Him, indeed, and were baptized, went to form the infant Church; but there was a clear distinction between those whom He specially selected to teach and preach and rule, and those who merely heard and believed and obeyed. The Church was constituted from the very first a hierarchical body, based upon the principles of order and authority. There were the teachers and the taught; the rulers and the ruled; the governors and the governed; the shepherds and the flock; the clergy and the laity. All were Christians; but there were diversities of gifts and operations (1 Cor. xii.; Eph. iv.). For clearness' sake let us forget at present about the ordinary faithful, and confine our attention to that class in the Church whom Our Lord entrusted with the preservation and propagation of His Gospel. They composed the Teaching Church—the "Ecclesia Docens," as theologians call it; it is to them and their successors we must look if we wish to know what God has revealed.

3. Well, the Lord endowed them with sublime powers. He made them priests. He gave them power to offer the Holy Sacrifice of the Mass (St. Luke xxii. 19). He gave them the power to forgive sins (St. John xx. 23). He made them His ambassadors, His messengers, His missionaries, His representatives. He bade them go and teach to others exactly what He had taught them. "Go," He said, "and teach all nations; teach them to observe all things whatsoever I have commanded you (St. Matt. xxviii. 19, 20). Go ye into the whole world and

preach the Gospel to every creature " (St. Mark xvi. 15). To ensure their success He promised them His Divine assistance: " I am with you all days, even to the consummation of the world " (St. Matt. xxviii. 20). He even communicated to them His own Divine authority, and compared their mission to His own Heavenly mission: " As the Father hath sent Me, I also send you " (St. John xx. 21). " He that heareth you heareth Me, and he that despiseth you despiseth Me " (St. Luke x. 16). And to crown all, their Master promised to preserve them from error in teaching His truth: He secured them from the possibility of falling into mistakes or of misleading others. " I shall be with you all days, even to the end of the world "; " The gates of hell shall never prevail against the Church "; " I shall send the Paraclete (the Third Person of the Blessed Trinity) from Heaven, when I am ascended, to confirm and complete what I have done. He will teach you all truth. He will bring all that I have taught to your remembrance; and He will even teach you more fully and clearly things which at present you cannot bear to hear " (St. John xiv. 26; xvi. 12, 13).

4. Now what, I ask, does all this mean ? It means that Jesus Christ made the Apostles and their successors His teaching Church to the end of time. I say their successors, for successors they must have if the Lord's design was to be carried into effect. If Our Lord desired that all men should have the opportunity of knowing the True Faith He must have willed the means to secure it; the Gospel must be perpetuated and preserved. Now, the Apostles were but mortal. They shared the common lot of men—death. But was the work of declaring God's Revelation to cease with them ? They had, therefore, to provide for the carrying on of this work after they were gone. They did so. They ordained Bishops to succeed them, men like SS. Timothy, Titus, Clement, and the rest, who formed the body of the episcopate under the headship of the Bishop of Rome, the successor of St. Peter.

They inherited the powers and the authority of the Apostles. They were the mouthpiece, the organ, and channel for conveying God's Revelation to men throughout all succeeding generations. Jesus Christ had given it to His Apostles; the Apostles handed it down to their successors; their successors to others, unchanged; and so has it been till the present hour, and will be till the end of the world.

Here was secured a regular, perpetual, teaching Body in every generation, representing in their corporate capacity Jesus Christ Himself, and speaking with His authority. All men were to listen and to believe. When they heard the voice of the Church, it was as if they heard the voice of Christ Jesus, for He spoke through her. She was endowed with infallibility—*i.e.*, divinely protected from teaching what was false, from changing, by one jot or tittle, aught of the original deposit, either by adding to or taking from it. She might (as she did) commit her Gospel to writing; or she might deliver it by tradition, handing it on from mouth to mouth, and from heart to heart, in unbroken succession. No matter, it was all the Truth of God. In merely human societies, indeed, error might easily creep in and corrupt the original doctrine, but never could that happen in the Church of God, the Spouse of Jesus Christ, His own Body, which He left on earth to be His representative among men. What kind of idea must people have of Our Lord who imagine that, after having constituted His Church our teacher, our mother, and our mistress in all that concerns our eternal salvation, He yet suffered her to fall into error and to teach us falsehood ?

This, then, is the plan that, as Catholics believe, Almighty God has taken to secure that all men, in every age, may know and believe the Revelation He made in Jesus Christ. Hear the Church, He says. Listen to her voice: it is My voice. I have set her up purposely that she may teach you the truths I have confided to her keeping. She can never lead you wrong, she can never fail, she can never err, for I Myself am protecting her. I send no angel from Heaven to teach you, no seraph, no saint, no spirit of departed Apostle or Evangelist. I give you the Church as your divine teacher; she knows all, she will tell you all: believe her and you are safe.

If it would not be considered irreverent, I might make clearer what I mean by a familiar illustration. Take the gramophone. You listen to a gramophone repeating, let us say, one of Caruso's songs. What has happened here ? Caruso sang that song; it was recorded and retained by an instrument, which reproduces it whenever required, and you say, " That is Caruso." So is it with the Catholic Church. Jesus Christ the Son of God spoke His Divine message to the Church; she has kept it all through, unaltered; and whenever we hear her declaring Christian doctrine we say: " That is the voice of Jesus Christ; that was what He said nineteen hundred years ago."

Surely now Our Lord's plan, as I have tried, however feebly, to explain it, must commend itself to all fair-minded people, even on natural grounds of practical common sense and expediency, as the very best suited for the end He had in view. It strikes us at once as obviously the most easy and effectual method of securing the safe transmission of His Revelation from one age to another. Who will fail to see at a glance its immense superiority over the method that Protestants fondly imagine Our Lord adopted—that of committing His Revelation, whole and entire, to a Book ? As a fact, He did no such thing, nor did the Apostles, as we have seen already. The notion is historically false and speculatively impossible. Who that considers all the circumstances calmly—the perishable nature of books and documents; their liability to change both in meaning and language in the course of centuries; the impossibility of ascertaining the true meaning of their contents; the danger of their perishing altogether—who, I ask, can cling to the absurd contention that

Our Blessed Lord, foreseeing all these and many other dangers and difficulties, and having other and better methods to choose from, yet deliberately chose one the most unsuitable and precarious, and entrusted His Revelation to no safer depository than the pages of a frail volume ?

5. But let us put this peculiar theory to the test of history and fact.   How did people who lived immediately after Our Lord's Ascension come to know His Revelation, His Gospel ?   By listening to the teaching of Apostle and Evangelist and Bishop.   St. Peter, St. Thomas, and the rest go forth, as they had been commanded, preaching the Gospel, telling the people exactly what Our Lord had told them, and being themselves witnesses of all that He had said and done for them.   The people listened and were converted.   Now it is St. Peter who converts them, now it is St. Paul, now St. Andrew, and so with the rest.   The New Testament itself, in the Acts of the Apostles, tells us something of the success of some of the Apostles; ecclesiastical history and tradition tell us the rest.   If anyone wished to learn the Christian Faith lately established, he said: " Let us go and listen to one of Christ's Apostles, or one of the Bishops they have ordained, or one of the priests or missionaries they have sent out "—in other words, let us hear the Church.   It was the same as though they heard Jesus Christ Himself.   Did they say, as it pleases the Protestant to imagine, " Let us ask for a New Testament ?"   But there was, as yet, *no* New Testament !

Well, it is the same at this day.   Does anyone, be he pagan, Jew, or heretic, wish to become acquainted with the Christian Faith ?   Let him hearken to the voice of the Catholic Church.   It is the same Body to-day as it was on the Day of Pentecost—larger, certainly, and more fully developed, as the tree is larger than the sapling, as the man is more fully developed than the boy; but nevertheless identically the same body.   She has the identical

Gospel to proclaim. She is the identical teaching body constituted by Our Lord. The Bishops have succeeded each other with identical order and jurisdiction in regular, unbroken line from the Apostles; ever in union with the Roman Pontiff, the Vicar of Christ; ever guarding jealously the Divine Deposit and preserving it from error or corruption. The Church is like a man gifted with perpetual youth, who lived with Our Lord, heard Him speak, received His doctrine, and has lived ever since, and is living now, to tell us with perfect recollection exactly what He taught. And so I listen to the Church now and I say: " That is the voice of the Teacher whom Jesus Christ appointed to teach in His Name until He shall come again." He does not mock us. If I believe the Church, then I cannot possibly go wrong. If He sent an angel from Heaven to instruct me, I should surely believe Him. If He sent me an Apostle or a saint from Heaven, surely I would believe him. Certain it is He sends me neither the one nor the other; but it is equally certain that He *has* sent me the Catholic Church as a Heavenly messenger and teacher, accredited and authorized above any angel or saint, to speak in His Name, and I can say with Richard of St. Victor: " Lord, if we are in error, by Thine own Self we have been deceived " *(de Trin.* i. 2). Shall I not be satisfied with this ? Shall I run after other teachers ? Shall I refuse to believe her ? If so, then, I may as well at once proclaim myself an infidel, and join with those who say in their heart, " There is no God."

6. Again, let us put the matter to the test. I live in a town where there are about a dozen and a half ministers, and I suppose two or three dozen preachers of sorts, all proclaiming what they call the Gospel. They hold forth in churches and halls, at street corners and in public parks, and, I believe, in private houses as well. Now, in this same town there came to the priest one day a man, who said: " For God's sake, tell me something about the Catholic religion. I have been through all the other

kinds, and I am no nearer the truth." Now, what exactly was the position of matters here? Here was a man who wanted to know the truth of God, the truth of Christ Jesus. He did not come to be converted to the Catholic Church; he was not asking for instruction with a view to becoming a convert; he simply wanted, first and foremost, to know the Christian Faith; in other words, to know and believe the truth revealed by Jesus Christ in order to save his soul. What happened substantially, then, was this— I shall draw it out at greater length for the sake of clearness:

He goes to a minister or a preacher and says: " Excuse me, sir, but what are you engaged in?" " I am preaching the Gospel of Jesus Christ," he is told. " But who gave you authority to speak for Jesus Christ?" he asks. The answer will depend on the position of the preacher.

1. Evangelist's Claim Examined.

Let us suppose he is an irresponsible evangelist, working on his own account. He will in all probability say: " The Lord sent me." " Prove it," says the inquirer. " Where are your credentials? Show me your testimonials; give me clear proof that Jesus Christ has really sent you to be His ambassador, to declare His Revelation." At once, of course, the man points to the Bible. " This Blessed Book," says he, " the Word of God, is my credentials." " My good sir," replies our inquirer, " that is no answer at all. The Bible proves nothing about *you* ; where do you find any passage in the Bible appointing *you* to expound the Gospel to *me*? Granting it *is* the Word of God, what right, what title have you to set yourself up as an authoritative and infallible interpreter of it to others?" " Oh, I I am not infallible." " Well, that is enough," replies my friend. " You will not do for me. I want somebody infallible. You are simply airing your own opinions."

" But I am a saved man, and——" " Perhaps you are,
and perhaps you aren't; it is a disputable point. In any
case, that is a purely subjective matter, which is not
capable of being demonstrated to anybody else; and,
therefore, is of no consequence to *me*." " And the Lord
has called me to tell sinners of His wonderful salvation." " Proof, my dear sir, proof," persists our inquirer,
" I have only your word for that. Can you work miracles,
for example ? Can you produce evidence like St. Paul
of your Heavenly call ? Have you letters-patent testi-
fying to your appointment ? I am afraid you are nothing
but a well-meaning fanatic. I do not wish to insult you.
I do not doubt for a moment that you are a most earnest
and zealous Gospeller; but after all that is not enough to
convince others of your Divine vocation to teach. It is
plain to me that you are only a self-constituted preacher
of certain stock phrases about salvation torn haphazard
out of the New Testament, without coherence or connection
with the rest. I ask once for all, can you, or can you not,
prove to my satisfaction that you have been authorized
to teach me or anybody else all that God has revealed ?"
" Oh, take that Book, and read it for yourself," says the
Gospeller handing over a Bible. " Of that," replies my
friend, " I can make neither head nor tail. I am no great
scholar. I cannot read very well. I cannot understand
the big, queer words. I can get nothing but confused
notions out of it. It is too difficult. Besides, to tell the
truth, I have no time to study it; what I want is someone
I can trust, to explain to me that and everything else that
Jesus Christ taught. I understand He chose a body of
men to go forth and teach the Gospel He brought from
Heaven. They were to ' teach all nations ' the truth He
first taught them, and He promised He would be with them
Himself all days, even to the end of the world. They
must be somewhere about, then, these men, or their
successors, if I could only find them. You evidently are
not one of them. Good-day."

2. Minister's Claim Examined.

To a Presbyterian minister our earnest inquirer next betakes himself. " Who sent you here," he asks him, " to instruct the people in the way of salvation ?" " The Church of Scotland," replies the minister. " I received my orders from the Auld Kirk." " Indeed, and how far does that carry you ? Can you trace your orders and mission back to the Apostles ? It all depends upon that. You profess to believe in the one holy, Catholic, and *Apostolic* Church. What right has your Church to stand up and claim to be the Church the Lord built upon the foundation of the Apostles and Prophets ? Explain your spiritual pedigree. Produce your ecclesiastical genealogy — or shall I do it for you ?

" You existed last century, I admit, and the century before that, and the one before that again—the seventeenth. Granted. And the sixteenth century ? Yes, partly. But come to the year 1560. You existed then, yes; but before that ? You can go no farther. You come to a blank wall. That was the year you started; before that there was no such Church of Scotland. You have come 1500 years too late to be the Church that Jesus Christ set up when He said: ' Thou art Peter, and upon this Rock I will build My Church.' How could your Kirk be the organ and mouthpiece of God's Revelation throughout all these centuries when it was as yet unborn ? What Apostle, what Martyr, what Doctor, what Saint of the Church would recognize your little sect—a thing of yesterday—as the lineal descendant of the Apostolic Church, the Early Church, the Medieval Church ? The very idea is laughable. As well say that a thorn-bush of a few years' growth is identical with the old oak-tree that stands overshadowing it. The fact is, sir, that you are doing in this town the very same thing as the street preacher and roving Gospeller, whom you so despise: venting your own views—or, rather, the views of John Calvin, your founder, so far as they agree with your own — upon the Bible. As for any authority or power bestowed by God upon you or your Kirk to declare to me without doubt or hesitation the whole Revelation made by Jesus Christ—you simply haven't got it. You are a brand-new modern society, started upon the principle of private judgment of one part of God's Revelation, the written Word. You are no guide to me. You can speak for nobody except yourself. Your doctrines are no more than ' guesses at truth,' which are scouted with derision by your neighbour in the next street. If the blind lead the blind, both shall fall into the ditch."

3. In despair, then, our earnest inquirer comes to the Catholic priest. There is no use troubling Protestant teachers further; he had asked for bread, and they gave him a stone. He has had enough of " opinions " and " private judgments," and " views," about Christianity. He wants something definite and conclusive and final. He wishes someone to speak to him " with authority, and not as the Scribes "; someone that will undertake boldly, and with infallible certainty, to unfold to him the whole scheme of salvation the Son of God brought from heaven; someone who will not only claim to be, but will prove decisively that he is, a teacher with a Divine Commission, a Representative and Ambassador of Jesus Christ, appointed to speak in His Name. Then his mind would be at rest.

How the Priest Satisfied Him.

" You ask me,"said the priest, " what authority I have to stand up here and teach people the way of Salvation ? I shall tell you where I get my authority. I shall give you clear and satisfying proof that I am no self-constituted preacher of Christianity, but one of those commissioned by Almighty God. Who sent me here? The Archbishop of Glasgow. And who gave him the right to do that? Who appointed him? The Pope. And pray who is the Pope? He is the Bishop of Rome. But who gave him the power to do all this? Almighty God Himself. Let me prove it. Pope Pius X. is the successor of Leo XIII., Leo XIII. succeeded Pius IX., Pius IX. succeeded Gregory XVI., and so on, right back in a straight line of 258 Popes in succession till we come to St. Peter, who was the first Pope, and whom Our Lord made Head of the Church when He said to him: ' Thou art Peter, and on this Rock I will build My Church. Feed My sheep, feed My lambs. To thee I give the Keys of the Kingdom of Heaven. And whatsoever thou shalt bind upon earth it shall be bound in Heaven; and whatsoever thou shalt loose on earth, it shall be loosed in Heaven ' (St. Matt. xvi. 18-19). Here Our Divine Lord appoints a visible Head of His Church on earth to be for ever continued in the person of St. Peter and his successors. Now, as his successors were Bishops of Rome (for St. Peter was first Bishop of Rome) it follows that the Bishop of Rome is for ever to be the Vicar of Christ and His Supreme Representative on earth. Hence I know exactly where I stand, and what authority I have, and where I get it from. There is no dubiety or suspicion whatsoever about the position of any priest in union with the See of Rome. He can trace his ecclesiastical pedigree, his spiritual family tree, right back to St. Peter, the first of that long line of Supreme Pastors of the Church to which Our Blessed Lord committed His Revelation for all time. You listen to my teaching, then, and you are listening not to the fads and fancies of human and, therefore, fallible teachers, however clever, but to the teaching of every Catholic priest throughout the world, and of all the Bishops, who have inherited it direct from Apostolic days and preserved it unchanged and uncorrupted. A priest is not airing his own private sentiments or opinions when unfolding Christian doctrine, but is the official spokesman of that Church which was, by a special act of creation, set up by God to be the organ of His Revelation to men. His voice is the voice of the historic Church of Christ, of the primitive Church, of the Church of the Apostles, of the Apostles themselves who drank in their instruction from the very lips of Jesus Christ Himself. We preach and teach to-day exactly the same doctrines that St. Peter and the Twelve and St. Paul taught, neither more nor less. The Gospel of the Church is, and must be, identically the same in every age, for the truth liveth and changeth not. Hear the Church, therefore, and you hear Jesus Christ: ' *Ubi Ecclesia ibi Christus* '—' He that heareth you heareth Me. If they will not hear the Church, let them be as the heathen and the publican.' Here, therefore, good sir, is your teacher, your Mother, your Mistress, sent from God. Listen, believe, obey. You will then know all that God wishes you to know. Except ye be converted and become as little children, you cannot enter into the Kingdom of Heaven."

It may seem suspiciously like the fictional ending: " They lived happy ever afterwards." But it is no fiction; it is a fact, that the man became, in due course, and remains, a stanch and edifying Catholic.

CHAPTER VIII

SOME OBJECTIONS CONSIDERED

I THINK now the statement of the Catholic position which has been given ought to enable Protestants to get rid of several difficulties they feel, quite sincerely, regarding us.

1. To begin with, it ought to prove to them that the faith of a Catholic is not the grovelling, degrading thing they seem to imagine. They pity us because (they say) we cannot and dare not "think for ourselves." We are cowards. We have thrown away our God-given powers of reason and judgment. We have to swallow all that the priest or, at least, all that the Pope, tells us, whether our reason approves it or not. Our thinking faculties are paralyzed. We have given ourselves over to intellectual bondage and spiritual torpor.

How absurd all this must seem after what has been said ! All that we do (as must be patent enough now) is to submit our judgment and conform our beliefs to the authority Almighty God has set up on earth to teach us; this, and nothing else. Could any Christian do less ? We should be rebels and blasphemers if we refused. We are slaves of Rome ? No; we are spiritual subjects of the Bishop of Rome, whom Jesus Christ appointed Head of the Christian Church, and the Spiritual Pastor and Teacher of all Christians. "Feed My sheep, feed My lambs." Acknowledging him as the spokesman for the Divine Founder of Christianity and the interpreter of His revealed will, we are bound to yield to his authority. The Divine Founder we have no longer with us in person, but we have one whom He invested with full powers to speak for Him, and for all practical purposes that is the same thing.   It is all one whether the King opens Parliament in person, or deputes the Prince of Wales, or one of his Ministers; whether he opens the General Assembly of the Kirk himself or sends his " trusty and well-beloved cousin," the Royal Commissioner.   Jesus Christ speaks through Peter, and Peter speaks through Pius X.   So far, then, from being debasing or dishonouring to our intellect, we consider the Catholic attitude to be the most beautiful and sublime act of homage to Our Divine Lord; we are honouring and adoring Him Who is the first and essential Truth.

Renouncing our own judgment !   Giving up our freedom !   Of course we renounce our own judgment when God has spoken; of course we give up our freedom to believe the opposite of what God teaches.   Protestants do the same.   A Protestant who believes in the Blessed Trinity because God has revealed it—does he not renounce his own judgment upon it ?   A Protestant who believes in Hell or in the Incarnation—where is his freedom to reject it, without sin ?   So, if God declares that the Blessed Virgin was conceived Immaculate, or that there is a Purgatory, or that the Holy Eucharist is the real Body and Blood of Jesus Christ, shall we say, " I am not sure about that.   I must examine it for myself; I must see whether it is true, whether it is Scriptural ?"   Let who will take upon themselves such a responsibility.

On matters, indeed, that Almighty God has been pleased to leave open questions, we are free to hold our own opinions, and there is a wide field here where discussion is not only permissible, but right and proper, and, it may be, even laudable.   Thousands of volumes have been written on such subjects by theologians and priests.   In such a sphere they have perfect liberty; the Church allows it.   Moreover, not only does the Church allow, but she gladly encourages, the wisest, the most devout and learned of her sons to undertake researches into the mysteries already defined to be doctrines of faith; not, of course, for the purpose of finding whether they are true, but for the purpose of explanation, instruction, edification; of discovering and unfolding to the faithful more and more the inexhaustible treasures of Heavenly truth that lie imbedded in any one of the articles of the Faith. The world has been enriched by whole libraries of Catholic theology—dogmatic, moral, ascetical, mystical, and the rest. To speak, then, of the intellect being paralyzed and of the spiritual faculties being deadened by the Romish system is simply ludicrous. Neither the religious literature of Protestantism, nor the finished product of their spiritual system as seen in the lives of its devotees, is to be mentioned in the same breath with that of the Catholic Church.

When we speak of private judgment, then, let us be quite clear as to what we mean; it has its uses and it has its abuses. Private judgment, in the sense of compiling a creed for yourself out of the Bible, of accepting this doctrine and rejecting that, of judging what should be and what should not be an integral part of the truth revealed by God—this, of course, is entirely forbidden, for it is directly contrary to the method of arriving at the truth instituted by Our Lord Jesus Christ. Do people imagine that the Son of God, having revealed a body of truth definite and explicit, eternal and unchangeable, left it to us to cut and carve, and to pick and choose here and there such bits of it as suited our taste? What the better should we be to-day, what advantage would the Incarnation have brought to us, if, after all, we were still floundering about in doubt and uncertainty?

Far other is the Catholic conception of Christ's mission. So soon as Our Divine Lord, speaking through the voice of His Church, solemnly declares, " This is My teaching: this is included in the Revelation I made to the Apostles " —what Christian, I ask, or rather, what man that fears

God, Christian or no, will dare hesitate to bow in acquiescence, and say, " O my God, I believe because Thou hast said it " ?   Where is the grovelling subserviency in this ? Where the intellectual slavery ?   As well might we call a man grovelling and cowardly who should suffer himself to be conducted by an experienced guide through the snows and glaciers of an Alpine mountain, or over the trackless desert waste; as well blame a child for clinging to its mother's hand in its journey through the dark and pathless forest.

The use of private judgment, on the other hand, in the sense of an inquiry into the " motives of credibility," and a study of the evidences for the Faith, to enable you to find out which is the one Church founded by Jesus Christ— this is permissible, and not only permissible, but strictly necessary for all outside the Fold who wish to save their souls.   But mark well: having once found the true Church, private judgment of this kind ceases; having discovered the authority established by God, you must submit to it at once.   There is no need of further search for the doctrines contained in the Christian Gospel, for the Church brings them all with her and will teach you them all.   You have sought for the Teacher sent by God, and you have secured him; what need of further speculation ?   Your private judgment has led you into the Palace of Truth, and it leaves you there, for its task is done; the mind is at rest, the soul is satisfied, the whole being reposes in the enjoyment of Truth itself, who can neither deceive nor be deceived.   " Be convinced," says Cardinal Newman in his great sermon, " Faith and Doubt "—" be convinced in your reason that the Catholic Church is a teacher sent to you from God, and it is enough."   " You must come to the Church to learn; you must come, not to bring your own notions to her, but with the intention of ever being a learner; you must come with the intention of taking her for your portion, and of never leaving her.   Do not come as an experiment, do not come as you would take sittings in a chapel or tickets for a lecture-room; come to her as to your home, to the school of your souls, to the Mother of Saints, and to the vestibule of Heaven."

2. Another thing that must now be plain to Protestants is this: Not only is our act of confidence and of blind obedience highly honouring to Almighty God, but it is at the same time most pleasing to Him as a proof of real humility of mind. A Catholic soul is a humble soul. He willingly submits his judgment on questions the most momentous that can occupy the mind of man—questions of religion— to an authority located in Rome. His sentiments, his inclinations, his tastes, even his studies may be drawing him the other way and prompting him to resist; but he refrains; he refuses to follow his own opinion; and even though it cost him a very great effort, he forces his intellect into entire assent to the judgment of the Church. " O my God !" he cries, " I am poor, weak, blind, and ignorant; Thou art the Infinite and Eternal Truth. I prostrate myself before Thy Divine authority." This is humility of a high order, as well as a great act of faith; it is the humility and faith of little children.

And it is found universally among living members of the Catholic Church; without it you could not lay claim to be a Catholic. Absolute, immediate, and unfaltering submission to the teaching of God's Church on matters of faith and morals—this is what all must give—the greatest Saints, the profoundest scholars, or the humblest of the faithful—even on matters regarding which they previously held a contrary opinion. God has spoken: " Let all flesh be silent at the presence of the Lord " (Zach. ii. 13). The dogma of the Immaculate Conception is a case in point. The oracle of God spoke, controversy was instantly hushed, and there was unwavering acquiescence; this is humility of intellect.

Protestants seem to imagine that strength of mind consists in criticizing and disputing Christian doctrine. Catholics, on the other hand, think that true nobility of

soul and greatness of mind are evidenced chiefly in believing mysteries above our capacity simply because the
Church enunciates them to us; in thinking as she thinks,
accepting what she accepts, and rejecting what she rejects.
We are under no illusion as to the meaning of true humility.
The world has a very different conception of this virtue
from what we have; indeed, it scoffs at it.   Now the vice
of intellectual pride is undoubtedly one of the most terrible
blots on the Protestant system.   Freedom to think as
you please—unrestrained and unfettered by any obliga-
tion to any superior authority—this is the very thing to
foster pride of mind; it is flattering to human nature, it
panders to the natural inclination of mankind to form their
own opinion about everything, and to stick to it, through
thick and thin.   In short, it makes a very god or a fetish
of the intellect.   Devotion, then, to this so-called liberty
of thought is a serious obstacle to a Protestant's conversion; so long as he maintains this attitude of mind, he
never can become a Catholic.   His soul is not disposed
to receive so great a grace: " God resisteth the proud, and
giveth grace to the humble " (St. Jas. iv. 6).   He must
first renounce his self-confidence, admit his liability to
error, and abandon himself unreservedly to the teaching
of that authority higher than any human authority,
" which is the Church of the living God, the pillar and
ground of the truth " (1 Tim. iii. 15).

To me there is nothing more beautiful than the childlike submission to the teaching of the Catholic Church on
the part of the greatest and wisest of persons.   I used to
be profoundly edified in Rome with the genuine humility
of all the learned and brilliant philosophers and theologians—and they were many—who taught in the colleges
and universities of the Eternal City.   Beyond all doubt,
they are among the finest and acutest intellects in the
Catholic Church; yet on matters of faith they are as docile
and obedient to the voice of authority as little children,
and would deem themselves rebels and reprobates if they

resisted it in any single point. Far grander and nobler, surely, this, than the proud self-assertiveness of lesser minds ! Not a scholar among them but is at least the equal, and in many instances vastly the superior, in intellectual endowments, of the foremost Protestant exponents in Great Britain; yet, because they avoid novelties and keep to the beaten track of Catholic tradition, the world outside knows little or nothing of them, and heaps its praise on those who allow their fancy to run riot, and set themselves to invent some new theology, and make havoc of the sacred Deposit of Revelation. O my God, let my portion be with the Saints and Doctors of Thy Church ! If I may not have their learning or their sanctity, let me share at least in their humility ! Let me die rather than doubt a single jot or tittle of the Catholic Faith ! I wish for naught but the simple faith of St. Teresa. " When nearing death, she thanked God, with great affection, for having placed her in His Church, and often repeated, with ardour, ' O Lord, I am a child of the Holy Catholic Church !' " Let me accept, in adoring faith, all that the Holy Roman Church believes and teaches, and the more adoringly, the less I comprehend it, and let me so believe till faith is lost in sight !

THE CONFIDENCE OF A CATHOLIC.

3. Then, again, the explanation I have given of the Catholic position will enable Protestants to understand how it is that Catholics are always so sure of their ground, so confident in their beliefs, so immovable in their faith. That they are all this, everyone admits: it is a cause of astonishment to them that are without. Our perfect tranquillity of mind, our sublime certainty of being in the right, contrasts so glaringly with the doubt and unbelief all around that no one can help being impressed by it. " You know both sides of the question," said a friend

to me one day; " you think your side is right now ?" " I do not think it," said I; " I know it is right." A Protestant says, " I think I am right; I hope I am "; but a Catholic says, " I know I am." Whence this confidence arises must be evident enough by now. It is because we recognize that the Church which we obey has Divine authority to teach. He Who gave her the commission to " teach all nations " was the Only Begotten Son of God, and it was His own authority with which He invested her. Now, if the Founder of the Catholic Church had been merely a man, however great and good and wise, we could not have had the same confidence either in Him or in anyone whom He sent to teach in His Name; we should not have had a perfect and absolute certainty; we should have felt disposed, as we certainly should have been entitled, to exercise our own judgment on any of His doctrines—for to err is human. Who, for example, would have accepted such a dogma as that of the Real Presence in the Blessed Sacrament from one endowed with a merely human intellect like our own ? But so soon as we discern in the Catholic Church an ambassador having authority, from Him Who is the uncreated and eternal Truth, to declare His Truth to men, then all difficulty vanishes: we bow our heads in adoring faith. Here is the secret of our confidence. This is why we are as certain of the truth of our doctrines as we are of our own existence, or of the truth that the sun shines and that the world is round. This is why we are certain, not only that our doctrines are true now, but that they are eternally and unchangeably true, as true as God Himself, and that they can never by any possibility be false. God has spoken them, and God cannot lie. This is why, if all the scientific men throughout the world held one doctrine, and the Church solemnly taught the opposite, we should believe the Church and disbelieve the scientists. This is why we defer with such profound reverence to the Decrees of the supreme ecclesiastical authority. The Vicar of Christ is the Vicar of

God; to us the voice of the Pope is the voice of God. This, too, is why Catholics would never dream of calling in question the utterance of a priest in expounding Christian doctrine according to the teaching of the Church; whilst, on the other hand, Protestants sit in judgment on their minister and accept only so much of his statements as they privately conceive to be correct. Who ever heard of anyone saying, " I believe all that the Presbyterian Church believes and teaches " ? or the Baptist Church, or the Methodist Church ? No one would be so stupid, for its authority is but human, and is no greater than that of the human beings who compiled its beliefs. And this, lastly, is why—whilst there is furious disagreement and controversy in the Protestant camp on every single point of Christianity, and they are all " tossed to and fro and carried about with every wind of doctrine "—in the Catholic Fold there is harmony, peace, unanimity; strong and deep and mighty as the ocean, yet calm as the un-rippled surface of the lake. It is the supernatural assent on the part of all the faithful to the Truth of God—" one Body and one Spirit; one Lord, one faith, one baptism, one God and Father of all, Who is above all and through all and in us all " (Eph. iv. 4, 6).

Sins against Faith.

4. Once more our Protestant friends will now under-stand how it comes about that for the Catholic conscience there exists a class of sins of peculiar gravity called " sins against faith," and that Catholics view them with such abhorrence. These sins are wilful doubt, disbelief, or denial of any article of faith. Wilfully and deliberately to entertain a doubt that any dogma of faith is not true, worse still to disbelieve it, and worst of all, explicitly to deny it—these are mortal sins; they constitute an offence against God that kills the soul by depriving it of the grace

of God, which is the supernatural life of the soul. And the reason is clear enough. Jesus Christ is God, and the Church is Christ's witness and representative to the world, the chosen messenger and exponent of His Divine Will and Word. Of this much a Catholic is absolutely certain. He is as sure of a truth when declared by the Catholic Church as he would be if he saw Jesus Christ standing before him and heard Him declaring it with His own Divine lips. The same consciousness of the Church's Divine authority—so admirably set forth in Monsignor Benson's " Christ in the Church "—runs through and dominates a Catholic's whole religious experience. If Jesus Christ, for example, were sitting in one confessional box, and a priest of the Catholic Church sitting in the next, a penitent would be as certain of the absolution of the priest as of that of Our Lord, for Our Lord has given His priest equal power. " He that heareth you heareth Me. As the Father hath sent Me, I also send you. Receive ye the Holy Ghost; whose sins you shall forgive, they are forgiven." It is from this very consciousness of the Church's authority that sins against the faith may arise for a Catholic. To doubt or deny the Church's word is all the same as doubting or denying Almighty God speaking to us; it is as though one should tell God to His very face: " I do not believe You." It is blasphemy and unbelief combined.

Now, a Protestant could hardly commit such a sin. Recognizing no fixed and final authority, like the visible Church and her supreme Head, he is free to believe whatsoever his own reason may commend to him. It is true, you may object, his authority is not reason, but God speaking through the written Word; but, after all, he reserves the right to interpret the Bible for himself, and with the " advance of science," and the " progress of truth," and " fresh discoveries," and " additional light," he may see reason to alter his interpretation, to change his beliefs. Hence it is that we find good Protestants at one stage of their career holding views quite different from those they held at a previous stage. From their point of view, that is perfectly consistent, and at each stage (for there might be several) they would claim to be equally faithful to their conscience and to the light they chanced to have at the time.

Thus, I repeat, it seems difficult (although theologically it is not impossible) to conceive of a Protestant being guilty of a sin against Divine faith; strictly speaking, he has no faith to sin against. This sin is really nothing more or less than resisting the supreme teaching authority. Catholics have such an authority and they may resist it; Protestants virtually have none outside their own judgment; and hence, whilst the former are taught to reject as a temptation of the devil and as an insult to Almighty God, any doubt or suspicion that may be suggested to them about the doctrines of the Catholic Church, Protestants are at liberty to consider any new idea on its merits, to discuss it and compare it with their present beliefs, and if it appear to them well-founded, they may adopt it as an improvement. Such is the difference between a man who holds the eternal, unalterable truths of Revelation, and the man who only weaves his own opinions.

The fact is that the whole conception of the Christian Faith, as a clearly defined body of truths, which we call the Deposit of Revelation, made known once for all by the Incarnate God to His Infallible Church—a body of truths so precisely fixed and determined that they could neither be increased nor diminished, and so eternally true that they could never be changed—this whole conception, I say, has simply perished from the average Protestant mind, and in its place he has set up the Bible, to be examined, investigated, criticized, turned upside down and inside out, with a view to constructing a system of Christianity approaching as nearly as possible to that which he is pleased to imagine was in the mind of Christ.

He may hold one belief this year and the opposite belief next year, but he will consider himself equally conscientious in both, though still remaining a member of the same sect. He may adhere to the Presbyterian creed for a time, then throw it over for the Unitarian, and finally embrace the Seventh Day Adventists, yet all the while reckon himself perfectly honest and sincere. He is conscious of no sin in so acting; indeed, he would have sinned had he done anything else! He must—so he says—be true to the light he receives; must follow " the leadings of the Spirit," must obey the Voice of Conscience. Thus, to save his soul, a Protestant in strict consistency follows a course of action which, if a Catholic pursued, would infallibly lead to his losing it.

CONVERTS AND PERVERTS.

5. And this explains the difference between the Protestant attitude towards a convert to the Catholic Church, and the Catholic attitude towards a pervert to Protestantism. In the former case the man, whether minister or layman, is considered to be only using his right of judging for himself. He has come, indeed—so his friends think—to a wrong conclusion. Still, that is a matter for his own conscience; he was entitled to use his right of private judgment and act accordingly; and he may be saved if he be true to himself. Moreover, there is no reason, in the nature of the case, why friendly relationships should be interrupted. That they are, unfortunately, sometimes interrupted is due, on the side of the Protestant, not to any spiritual anxiety for the seceder, or genuine theological zeal, or solicitude for God's honour, but to a vague " horror of Popery " in their midst in any shape or form, and to a feeling that the man is now a disgrace to his family and a discredit to his friends.

Catholics, on the contrary, can never approve or excuse the secession of any of their number to a false religion.

They know, for certain, he has taken a false step; that he has gone wrong; that he has abused his God-given reason; that he has culpably lost the gift of faith; that he has thrown away the pearl of great price; that he has left the city of peace for the city of confusion; that he has insulted God, wronged the Church, and scandalized the faithful; and as a rule they will feel obliged—and very properly so —to show their detestation of such apostasy by a marked change in their relationship towards him. Otherwise they would seem to condone his act and encourage Indifferentism.

Sin of a Heretic.

Here, before we leave this point, it will not be out of place to observe how ridiculous it is for Protestants to speak of " heretics " and " heresy " within their own communion, and to call the conversion of any of their members to the Catholic Church " apostasy." That is simply borrowing words from Catholic terminology which, apart from the Catholic Church, are utterly meaningless. Heresy and apostasy presuppose a fixed, irreformable creed, guarded by an infallible authority, residing in a body formed by Our Divine Lord to be the One Ark of salvation for all, and into which all, like Noah and his family, must enter if they would be saved. But nothing of this kind is to be found in Protestantism. Undoubtedly every society, whether civil or religious, has the right to censure, and even to expel, any of its members whom it may discover to be unfaithful to its rules. But to call the man's infringements, in the case before us, " heresy," and to brand the man himself as a " heretic," is supremely nonsensical. People are coming to laugh at the idea. " After all," they say, " if our Protestantism is based on private judgment, then we have the right to exercise it, and to interfere with it is to interfere with our most sacred liberties. Let us not forget, whether we be

Anglicans or Presbyterians, that we admit particular Churches may err, 'as the Church of Jerusalem, Alexandria, and Antioch have (*sic*) erred,' even in matters of faith; 'the purest Churches under Heaven are subject both to mixture and error,' and ' General Councils may err, and sometimes have erred, even in things pertaining to God ' (Thirty-nine Articles, xix, xxi. Confession of Faith, chapter xxv.). How, then, can we who proclaim our own fallibility, with any show of consistency, condemn one of our brethren for heresy ?" It is significant of the change that has come over Protestantism that there has been no heresy-hunt (as they call it) among the Kirks for many years; and, with the widening of their formulæ, so as to embrace clergy of all ways of thinking, the likelihood of another trial for heresy is a prospect exceedingly remote.

In the Catholic Church, on the other hand, heresy will always be possible, and a heretic will always be a real sinner. In Catholicism there exists an authority against which the self-willed may rebel, and a restraint upon the intellect against which the proud may chafe. A Catholic from his earliest years knows perfectly well what he is bound to believe, under pain of grievous sin; what Almighty God requires of him to believe. He knows the boundaries beyond which he dare not pass without finding himself in the midst of lies and errors. He knows where God's eternal and revealed truths end, and where pious opinions may begin. Above all, he knows—none knows as he knows—what is truth and what is falsehood in the clash of creeds around him; with unerring instinct, and at a glance, he can distinguish human inventions from the " Faith once delivered to the saints."

Such a man, therefore, may fall, may sin against faith; but only such a man. With such knowledge, with such light, with a conscience so formed, he may rebel; he may deny God's Truth; he may flout God's authority; he may turn his back on the Catholic Faith and on the Catholic

Church; he may cut himself off from the Body of Christ as men cut a branch off a tree. But, if he does, he knows what he is doing; he does it with his eyes open; he does it wilfully, deliberately, knowingly. Here is the terrible malice of his heresy, his apostasy, or his schism: he sins in the full light: he lifts up his hand against the Most High God. He knows God has not changed, and that still as before he is bound to receive the Church's authority as the authority of God. But he refuses. Like Lucifer, he says, " I will not serve; I will not obey "; and perhaps

> " When he falls, he falls like Lucifer,
>   Never to hope again."

Great, indeed, is the fall, great the loss, great the punishment; great, then, must be the horror in every Catholic breast at such a fall, and greater even the sorrow for a brother plunged from light into the darkness.

> " So fallen! so lost! The light withdrawn
>   Which once he wore."

Joining in False Worship.

6. One further difficulty which Protestants feel about our way of acting will now, it is hoped, have been cleared up. Catholics are blamed as bigots for not attending Protestant services, while Protestants make no scruple about attending a Catholic service. Many years ago, being still a minister of the Kirk, I remember a young person saying to me, " Is it not a curious thing that the Catholics in our work will never come to our church, though we go with them sometimes to the chapel ?" " The reason," I answered, " seems fairly obvious. They believe they have all the truth in their Church, and do not need to go elsewhere in search of it: whilst we believe that truth is scattered here and there in all the Churches, and we go wherever we think we shall hear it preached." It was not, indeed, a very theological answer, but consider-

ing the inchoate condition of my ideas about Catholicism
at the time, it might pass as fairly correct so far as it went.

I may improve upon it now, and say that the primary
reason for holding the attitude we do is (1) we are forbidden to take part in false worship. Protestantism is
false, and therefore as it stands is a sin against faith, in
which we may have neither part nor lot.   That it contains some elements of truth, no one of course will dream
of denying; otherwise it could never have survived at all;
whatever it carried away from the Catholic Church when
it started in the sixteenth century is necessarily true.
The same thing may be said of Mahommedanism and
Confucianism and Hinduism and any other religion yet
discovered. Some fragments of the truth they must
possess, although in some the truth is overlaid and buried
beneath such a mass of falsity and corruption that its
influence is hardly felt at all.

Again, it must be admitted that in all religions, there are
multitudes of people who are in good faith, and not only
are they in good faith, but they are actually good, according to their lights, living good lives, and following whatsoever things are true, honest, just, lovely, and of good
report.   But to admit that is by no means the same thing
as to admit that their religion is true.   Take Protestantism.   The system in fact is false, and the goodness to be
found in thousands of its adherents exists in spite of the
falsity of the system.   Whatever is good in it is due either
to those natural truths implanted by Almighty God in the
hearts of all men alike—" the law written in their hearts,"
as St. Paul calls it (Rom. ii. 15)—or to those scraps of
Revealed truth borrowed from Catholicism.   To the
operation of any exclusively Protestant tenets no goodness
can possibly be attributed. Hence we may truly say
that if a Protestant is good in the supernatural order, it is
owing to the Catholic influence inhering in his religion; and
if he be saved, he is saved in so far as he was a Catholic at
heart.   He belongs to the soul of the Catholic Church,

though not to its visible body; he is, as theologians would say, a Catholic " in voto." A good Protestant is always better than his creed, while a good Catholic can never be better than his. Protestantism, then, as a system—no matter which section of it you may take, whether Presbyterianism or Anglicanism or any other—is false. We may admire and respect thousands of its adherents; we may cherish a warm personal affection for many most estimable individuals amongst them, and even prefer them in many respects to some of the " household of the Faith ": yet, considered as a scheme of Christianity, a guide to salvation, a system of theology or of morals or Church government, or of anything else, it must be pronounced as an apostasy, an offence to Almighty God, and as such must be condemned without reserve. And this, I repeat, is the fundamental reason why Catholics are forbidden to have anything whatsoever to do with it. We believe that we are obliged to worship the one living and True God, not in any way we like, but in the way that He wishes— not in any fashion we please, but according to the form He has been pleased to reveal; and I am sure that Protestants themselves no less than Catholics would judge it to be a great sin to countenance or participate in a religious worship which they were persuaded was displeasing to their God and Saviour.

(2) But there is another reason for our attitude towards Protestant services. I say nothing for the present about the scandal that might be given to other Catholics, or the false impression that might be left on the minds of non-Catholics, or the harm that might conceivably be done to the man's own faith by attending heretical meetings. One thing alone that would make his presence both unnecessary and absurd is this, that in the Catholic Church he already possesses the truth, and the whole truth, of God, and that outside the pale of Rome there is not a scrap of additional truth of Revelation to be found. This arises from the fact, to which I have so often alluded, of

the Catholic Church being the sole depositary of the Faith revealed by God the Son in His Incarnate Life. Every true dogma as to faith and morals, every true form of spirituality—dogma unmixed with error, and spirituality unspoiled by fanaticism—exists within her wide embrace.   Divine Science and heroic sanctity flourish in all their beauty side by side—or rather the one springs from the other; and never in her long history could it happen that the Church borrowed aught from another. What possible benefit, then, could a Catholic derive from a Protestant service ?   What is new, he will not have; and what is true he can learn, and learn far better, from his own mother and mistress the Catholic Church.   He is content with what he has, he desires nothing more, and he is consoled by the thought that all the Heavenly treasures of grace and of wisdom are to be found within her bosom, and that generation after generation they are brought forth by her own children, at once a pure offering to Almighty God, their Creator and their Source, and a striking demonstration to the world that she alone is the one true Church of Jesus Christ.

CHAPTER IX

A CONCLUDING APPEAL

AND here I conclude. Let me sum it all up in a word. What have we seen? We have seen the absolute necessity of faith if we would be saved. We have seen that faith consists in believing whatsoever God has revealed, and because He has revealed it, Who can neither deceive nor be deceived.

And we have seen, lastly, that we are to learn all that God has revealed by the testimony, teaching, and authority of the Catholic Church. Oh, beautiful, merciful, easy is the provision of the good God for our salvation! " He that spared not even His own Son, but delivered Him up for us all, how hath He not also with Him given us all things?" Will men not listen to Him when He cries unto them? Will they not follow the path He points out to them? Faith cometh by hearing; but how shall they hear without a preacher? The preacher sent by God is the Catholic Church. " He cannot have God for his Father who hath not the Church for his mother."

May I now repeat an appeal already spoken to those who as yet know her not, to those who as yet are afraid of her because they do not understand her? The Catholic Faith satisfies the uttermost longings of the human soul; it gives peace to the intellect because it is really God in the Catholic Church that satisfies us—God brought to us and feeding us with His Truth, with Himself, with His own Body. Little do they know of that fair and beautiful Spouse of

Christ who imagine that its members are deluded with a false security, a hollow peace, an artificial repose; that their minds are, as it were, asphyxiated, soothed into a kind of precarious and unwholesome lethargy; that their wills and their intellect enjoy no true and solid satisfaction, but are leaning upon some humanly invented and delusive saviour outside Jesus Christ altogether. I know that this is what many earnest people who wish our Lord to be known and loved and believed really imagine about us Catholics. And oh, that they who think such things could only know the " joy and peace in believing " as we do ! Nothing, let me assure them, but our dear Lord and Saviour Jesus Christ, true God and true Man, could ever give repose or certainty to the troubled heart. No rites and ceremonies, no saints or angels, no external beauty or fascination, could ever by themselves satisfy the soul of any Catholic. These would in themselves be less than nothing and vanity, and all the gorgeous and ravishing attractiveness of the Catholic Church would be but a hideous and a barren mockery, were it not that the Eternal God and Saviour dwells in the midst of her, and gives a meaning and life to them all. They exist for His sake, and honour Him, and reflect His beauty; but He Himself it is, and nothing less than He, on whom the affection and faith of our hearts are fixed. " Thou hast made us for Thyself," as St. Augustine beautifully says, " and our souls are restless till they find rest in Thee."

Just as the essential glory and happiness of Heaven is the Presence of God Himself, and without Him all else, however beautiful, would only sicken and delude us, so in the Kingdom of Heaven on earth—which is the Catholic Church—it is Jesus Christ Our Lord, the Lamb slain, that constitutes our joy and peace. He is ever with us, loving us so much that He has chosen to abide with us in the Blessed Sacrament, night and day, receiving the loving adoration of legions of angels and of millions of human souls throughout the world. He it is and He alone that has so inflamed the hearts of saints that they have had to cool their breast at a fountain of water, lest they should be altogether consumed with the fire of Divine Love. He it is, and He alone, that has drawn saints into such ecstasies of love and union with Him that, like St. Paul, they could say they had been " rapt even to the third heaven and heard unutterable words." He it is, and He alone, that has often appeared to holy priests at Mass under the sweet figure of a little child. Could our Protestant friends but know how we love Jesus and how Jesus loves us, and how the livelong day and night there is never an hour, never a moment, in which He is left without adorers " in spirit and in truth "—whether in silent cloister or lonely chapel or gorgeous cathedral—they would surely cry aloud: " In Judea God is known." " As the hart panteth after the fountains of waters, so panteth my soul after Thee, O God." So echoes the Catholic soul, and in His lovely dwelling-place upon earth we find Him at all times and at any time giving peace in our troubles, joy in our sorrow, consolation in our distress, perfect repose of mind and will and intellect, peace which the world can neither give nor take away. We receive Jesus Christ, and we are satisfied; satisfied so far as we can be out of Heaven. It is the privilege of the noblest, the mightiest, the richest, but it is also the privilege of the poor and lowly, the unlettered and despised, that they may not only approach Our Lord and touch the hem of His garment, but receive Him into their very breast, and lavish upon Him their heart's affection, and be united to Him and repose upon His bosom. Yea, so true is this that those who have literally nothing of this world's goods, and none to comfort them, and nothing to lean upon for enjoyment or pleasure, nor even perhaps the bare necessaries of life— these, I say, God's poor, yet find in Jesus all they need, and with Him fear no ill. " My beloved to me, and I to mine ": and even in the Valley of the Shadow of Death, they are calm and confident and happy, for they know that some day, perhaps it may be very soon, Him whom they loved and received under the Sacramental Veils they will see face to face, and will dwell with Him for ever in that Temple where the Lamb of God Himself is enthroned in glory, and where there shall be no more death, neither sorrow nor crying, neither shall there be any more pain; and God shall wipe away all tears from their eyes.

Separated brethren ! Our prayer for you is that you may one day share with us that glory and that joy. Nothing but your own wilful deafness to the voice of the Good Shepherd will keep you out of it. " To-day if you will hear His voice, harden not your hearts." Think, study, pray, that you may do God's Holy Will, that you may have light to see the Truth, and strength and courage to embrace it, for, as it has been said, " it is a rare gift to be a Catholic " (Newman). And if, in pursuing the path of duty at the call of God, you are called upon like them of old, to " leave your people and your father's house," fear not, and shrink not. " He that loveth father or mother more than Me is not worthy of Me," and " he that doth not take up his cross daily and follow Me cannot be My disciple." You will then be going forth, not, like Abraham, into a strange country, knowing not whither you are going, but into that " city which hath foundations, whose builder and maker is God "—the Holy Catholic Church. You will be only making the sacrifice which thousands have made before you, and you will enter upon the same reward. You will be recompensed beyond your wildest dreams for all you have abandoned. You will be leaving the Babel of Confusion for the City of Peace, doubts and torments for calm and tranquil joy, the un-certainties and contradictions of human error for the truths and certainties of Almighty God. You may have given up all, but you have gained the Pearl of Great Price, for you will have the knowledge and love of God here below, together with the assurance of His Blessed Presence for all eternity in Heaven: " Everyone that hath left house, or brethren, or sisters, or father, or mother, or wife, or children, or lands for My name's sake shall receive an hundredfold, and shall possess life everlasting " (St. Matt. xix. 29).